"

Having followed Nigel's investment advice for many years implementing the concepts of Evidence Based Investing as espoused in this book. I found the book to be compelling and one I will be encouraging, wholeheartedly, my adult children to read and follow the investment principals, in a discipline way to help achieve their financial goals.

Ray Osborne, retired Partner of
ASX 200 financial services company

I met Nigel Baker in 2004 when on his ascendancy in one of Sydney's prestigious wealth firms. My firm was piloting a new program for financial services professionals with about twenty firms. Though youngest in the group, Nigel was a standout. That program of 2004 still runs today with thousands of advisers from hundreds of Australian wealth firms having attended. In many ways I have been lucky to learn more from Nigel Baker than he has learned from us. Nigel's book provides the frameworks to understand that money in only one part of a better financial life. It will help ensure the required focus of all factors that create better financial lives, not just the money aspect.

Jim Stackpool, Managing Director,
CERTAINTY ADVICE GROUP

What I really want to discover and pass down to my successive generation is smart, savvy and simple – a disciplined and rational approach to investing and wealth creation. This book is my blueprint.

Christian Lane-Brown, MedTech Consultant,
Boston Scientific

I've had the pleasure of knowing Nigel for over 30 years. Initially it was through our love of sport and Rugby but more recently through Investment and Wealth management. Nigel possesses high standards, discipline, work ethic, integrity and vast experience in Wealth Management. This book reflects his great ability to provide clarity and practical investment advice in plain English for us all to understand and implement.

Stirling Mortlock AM, former Captain of the Australian Rugby Team

Nigel is one of those rare professionals who can provide clear, practical and sound advice for the non-expert.

As an independent, you know Nigel is on your side. His playbook on how to build wealth with confidence and without hassle is a gift for everyone who worries they may not have the future plan they need.

Mark Hodgson, Author, Speaker and Business owner

If you read one book on investing this year, make *The Super Secret* the one. Nigel's practical and insightful approach to investing and wealth management really opened my eyes to some of the investment myths I've been believing for too long. Well worth the read.

Justin Simpson BSc LLB – Patent Attorney & Entrepreneur

The SUPER Secret

NIGEL BAKER

General Advice Warning

The information contained within this publication is general in nature and does not take into consideration any objectives, financial situation or needs.

Before you consider whether to acquire any financial product you should firstly obtain and read the relevant Product Disclosure Statement.

ISBN: 978-1-922409-66-9
Published by Vivid Publishing
A division of Fontaine Publishing Group
P.O. Box 948, Fremantle
Western Australia 6959
www.vividpublishing.com.au

 A catalogue record for this book is available from the National Library of Australia

Contents

About Nigel

Over the past 20 years Nigel has worked as a chartered accountant and certified financial planner advising clients. He has worked for some of the largest global institutions, was a partner in one of Australia largest Accounting groups, and then started his own advisory practice in 2012 Arch Capital named after his second son Archie.

Determined to deliver open, evidenced-based financial advice Nigel started his own independent private wealth business, Arch Capital in 2012.

Wanting to also provide access to younger and not so complex clients to evidence based investing, Nigel also founded Scientiam in 2020, www.scientiam.com.au an online portal that provides access to knowledge from decades of academic research to help individuals become smarter investors – essentially the information the investment industry doesn't want people to know about.

Nigel has seen the best and worst of the industry first hand and, fortunately, came across the evidence based way to invest early his career . Evidence based investing is an investment approach that uses science rather than guesswork, focuses on what you can control as a client, and most importantly puts the client first.

Nigel is passionate about ensuring advice is independent and the client comes first.

It's Nigel's mission to empower people to take control of their own financial future by sharing what the investment industry doesn't want you to know. You don't have to pick stocks or gamble to increase your chances of investment success.

Contrary to the way most manage their money, decades of research shows us all that if we follow certain principles you don't actually need to worry about or watch markets daily - and you will have a better investment experience and higher chance of "beating the market".

Introduction

"The difficulty lies, not in the new ideas, but in escaping from the old ones." John Maynard Keynes

It's time investors came first and were able to access the truth about investing.

There has been a big shift in thinking in global markets, and you have to know about it to successfully invest and manage your investments.

The Super Secret has been written to help you understand the facts, give you access to unbiased knowledge and show you where to find information so you can invest smarter and secure a better future.

I want all Australians to have this knowledge, so they have a structure to make the best investment decisions using evidence and facts from decades of academic research.

This book will show you a new way forward, where your money looks after you first and foremost.

We are all investors and this book is written for you, to explain investment markets so you find out how they really work and how to use this knowledge to ensure you have the best possible chance of success.

As soon as we start working, we earn money. Whether you use your money wisely can make a huge difference to the quality of your life forever.

To be a successful investor, it is important to gain information, to have a process, and to focus on what you can control. In this book, I explore ideas from some of the leading minds in finance so you can start your journey to a different and better way to invest. Let's use these ideas to achieve your goals.

A survey by Russell Investments in January 2020 found that 67 per cent of respondents did not know how their super was invested and 21 percent were unaware they could choose their own investments.

The problem with the investment industry is that it's too focused on the short term, and it puts itself first. To make money out of you, many asset managers and institutions promise higher expected returns or some "secret". They have to do this because they won't be around for as long as the investment markets, so they need your money now.

I have written this book to provide you with detailed specialist knowledge to help you invest better, but of course this is just the beginning for you and future generations of Australians.

I'm not giving you hot tips or get-rich-quick schemes. This book is to help you set up an investment process using evidence from decades of academic research to give you the best chance of success.

This book shares the truth about investing and shows you how to find publicly available information that has been around for decades, but you may not know about.

Investing does not need to be complicated. While there are thousands of different shares and sectors in each market, the message I want to share with you is that most of your returns (dividends and share price growth over time) come more from the asset class you are in than the individual shares (security) you own.

- Focus on what you can control and let the markets work for you.
- Let's use the leading minds of finance to help you achieve your goals.
- I am sure you will enjoy this journey.
- My goal is to ensure you have an investment experience that puts you first.

1

It's Your Money, Manage It Well

"To invest successfully does not require a stratospheric IQ, unusual business insights, or inside information", Warren Buffett says in the foreword to Benjamin Graham's 'The Intelligent Investor'. "What's needed is a sound intellectual framework for making decisions and the ability to keep emotions from corroding the framework."

All Australians are or will be investors. For many this is by default via your superannuation fund. Your compulsory savings of 9.5 per cent of your salary are being invested by your superannuation fund in banks, mining, health care and infrastructure operations — roads, ports, airports, telecommunications and electricity distributors.

You may also become an investor by receiving an inheritance, buying a property or saving for a holiday.

You may dream about buying a boat, travelling the world or taking a cruise. All these goals require investing. The better an investor you are, the better your life will be.

Money is important to you for different reasons than to me, and we will all have different amounts of money at various times of our lives. How we manage this money to provide the outcomes we seek for ourselves and those we care about is very important.

While many people understand that their superannuation fund invests in shares, you may also have investments in bonds, cash, property and even private equity, options, and unlisted assets such as infrastructure. Many of these investments have names and descriptions you are not familiar with: terms like 'dividend', 'yield', 'franking credit', 'hybrids', 'return of capital', 'return on equity', 'capitalisation', 'Dow Jones', 'All Ordinaries' mean absolutely nothing to many Australians. These mysterious terms and jargon have helped keep investment the domain of your investment managers, safe from you ever taking control or knowing enough to be sufficiently confident to make a change.

Do you really know what you are invested in? Do you really know what you should and, more importantly, what you should not be invested in?

You are not alone if you answered no. Very few people do know. Yet your superannuation and investments have the ability to enhance your life, to enable you to live your dreams and do the things you really want to do!

It is important you have the knowledge and skills to know if your money is being well managed, but it's not a subject that is taught at school. Financial literacy in Australia is very low, despite our relatively high level of education.

As personal finance is not taught, it is no surprise that most investors make the same mistakes, such as trying to pick stocks or time markets, and try to buy in the highs and sell in the lows.

The Education Index, published with the UN's Human Development Index in 2015, listed Australia as 0.939, the highest in the world. Since 2010, the Education Index has been measured by combining average adult years of schooling with expected years of schooling for children, each receiving 50 per cent weighting.

2015 Education Index[5] [hide]

Rank ◆	Country ◆	Education Index ◆	Expected years of schooling ◆	Mean years of schooling ◆	HDI rank ◆	Continent[6] ◆
1	Australia	0.939	20.4	13.2	2	Oceania
2	Denmark	0.923	19.2	12.7	5	Europe
3	New Zealand	0.917	19.2	12.5	13	Oceania
4	Norway	0.916	17.7	12.7	1	Europe
5	Germany	0.914	17.1	13.2	4	Europe
6	Ireland	0.910	18.6	12.3	8	Europe
7	Iceland	0.906	19.0	12.2	9	Europe
8	United States	0.900	16.5	13.2	10	North America
9	Netherlands	0.897	18.1	11.9	7	Europe
10	United Kingdom	0.896	16.3	13.3	16	Europe

Image source https://financial capability.gov.au

Do you really know how to invest? Do you have access to the truth about how markets work?

It is possible to demystify investing and demonstrate the truth so that you can have an investment philosophy that puts your interests first and prioritises you the client before anything else.

The difference between a poor investment and a great one is huge, and having a sensible investment philosophy that you stick to over time will make a huge difference to your life.

Whether you are 16 and have just started your first job at McDonalds, have just retired, or are 85 years old, investing is important. You are never too young or too old to learn something new. While it helps to start investing younger, it's never too late to get going.

While some people think that you need to be rich to be a successful investor, or have access to the best investments, this is not true. There are many successful investors and wealthy people who started small. And there are many very wealthy people who have bad investments, or who make money in business but then invest in dumb ideas or hand their money over blindly to others to invest.

I made some bad investing mistakes when I was young. I remember investing in a tip from a friend during the tech boom of 2000/2001 and losing a few thousand dollars. But if I'd simply invested that money in the manner I now know works, and which this book explains, and paid regular instalments, that few thousand would be almost $100,000 today.

Instead it's worth zero. If only I'd known then what I know now!

From my own Mum's experience to that of the many clients I have worked with over the past 20 years, I want to share stories and experiences to help you avoid some simple mistakes and lead you to an investment approach backed by decades of academic and Nobel prize-winning research that will give you a much greater chance of success.

This research is publicly available and has been for decades.

Is there a higher priority than ensuring you know how to invest properly for your future?

With the rising costs of living in basic groceries, health services and house prices added to our longer life expectancy that strain on governments, it is important that all

Australians do what they can to learn how to be as financially independent as possible.

The reality is that most Australians have not had any education in investing or finance, and don't have access to honest independent resources. Unfortunately, what they do have access to for investment decisions are industry marketing, advertising and media reports .

And it's even worse than that, as we have discovered through the Royal Commission into Financial Services: banks and their sales people have not acted in their clients' best interests. They have acted in their own interests both at a personal and a corporate level so they were conflicted when it came to providing advice to their clients. It's not only the banks which have been at variance. Many large super funds and industry funds, accountants and brokers have also been questioned on whether they have been putting the end customers' interests first.

As a result of this, and a confusing investment, tax and superannuation system, most investors end up doing exactly the opposite of what they should be doing.

There is, thankfully, plenty of independent, peer reviewed research dating back to the 1950s on how best to invest. The leading minds in finance have looked into this challenge for the benefit of us all, and the findings are remarkably consistent: there is a different and better way to invest.

These Nobel-winning findings and evidence are widely known in academic circles, but the problem remains that the investing public – you – remains largely unaware of them and no one has made much effort to inform you.

The primary reason for this is that many investment advisers, industry commentators and so-called experts are either unaware of this research or choose to ignore it. Or I can be cynically blunt and say there is no benefit to them if they tell you about it.

As an independent investment adviser, I have battled to communicate this story to my clients for over 20 years. Battled because, despite being widely researched and validated by decades of academic research, very few advisers have implemented this approach in Australia. Very few 'experts' in the press address this evidence sensibly. Evidence-based investing is not sexy for the media, and the philosophy of those designing the investment products (and that's all they are) has been to train their salespeople to sell on commission.

My role has been and continues to be to simply work for clients and ensure their investments are the best possible for them.

It is my professional obligation to put my clients' best interests first. I am grateful to have come across a firm by the name of Dimensional Fund Advisors early in my career, and learned this fundamental ethical, and now legal, obligation via my chartered accounting exams and experience.

I was introduced to Dimensional in 2001 simply because they never have and never will pay commissions to induce 'advisers' to sell their products. In the investment industry this was and is unusual and refreshing. I was a fee-only adviser — very rare in 2001! I went to meet Dimensional with my then boss. The fee-only model has influenced my whole career, although the fee-only approach has not been an easy one to market, because the industry does a great job of convincing you that their high-cost, commission-loaded products are better. And they have way larger marketing and advertising budgets. In my previous roles, investment committees disapproved of the concept because it did not pay upfront commissions, and peers ridiculed it as if it were some type of cult. Sometimes the right way can be more difficult, but it has been worth the effort and endeavour.

The vital principle underpinning my fee-only path has been the continual search for what is best for my clients. If you truly put your clients first, then this is the only way for advisors to implement portfolios and give clients the best chance of success, and also to apply appropriate governance as a trusted fiduciary with the responsibility of managing peoples' money.

If you are using an adviser who does not use a fee-only strategy, it's time to start again. In my view, this means they are not working simply for you: they are putting their own ego and interests before yours, making decisions based on the commission they will receive.

There are billions of dollars invested through a fee-only approach globally, although it's a fairly small segment of the investment market in Australia due to the banks having controlled the market for so long and many advisers coming from sales roles in banks rather than being guided by professional principles.[1] Banks have an important role

---

1 Many regulations have been introduced recently to try and improve the standard of advice in Australia, the latest being the Financial Adviser Standards and Ethics Authority (FASEA) requirements aiming to improve educational standards.

in our system but, as we know, they do not do a great job in providing financial advice because they put their own interests before yours.

This book shows a better way to invest: one that puts you, the client, first.

Before I get to the investment philosophy and the 'how', it's important to understand why being a better investor is so important.

There are 10 key reasons why you should understand the facts about investing, and how that can make a big difference to your life.

CHAPTER 1 SUMMARY

» With trillions of dollars invested in superannuation, isn't it time we all took more interest in our money?
» Australia is an intelligent country by many standards, however we have very poor financial literacy
» Most Australians know very little about how their superannuation is invested.

2

10 Reasons why You Need to Manage Money Successfully, and why You Need to Start now

"The number of managers that can successfully pick stocks are fewer than you'd expect by chance. So, why even play that game? You don't need to." David Booth

Reason #1. To save for a house

Many people start work and, after a few years, decide that renting is no longer for them. It is still the Australian dream to own your own home, even though over the past 20 years the cost of housing has increased dramatically. It is harder now than ever to save the deposit required, but at the same time interest rates are at historic lows, so there is a trade-off. Even so, the median house price in many Australian capital cities is $809,349[2]. In the chart below we list the median prices across all major cities:

---

2 Source: Domain House Price Report, December Qtr 2019.

STRATIFIED MEDIAN HOUSE PRICE

Capital City	Dec-19	QoQ Change	YoY Change
Sydney	$1,142,212	5.7%	6.8%
Melbourne	$901,951	5.0%	8.7%
Brisbane	$577,664	1.3%	1.5%
Adelaide	$542,947	1.3%	1.1%
Canberra	$788,621	7.3%	5.4%
Perth	$537,013	0.7%	-1.9%
Hobart	$530,570	8.5%	15.6%
Darwin	$509,452	-3.0%	-1.1%
National	$809,349	4.2%	5.5%

To save for a house you can no longer just invest in cash, because all you get is a return of 0.25 per cent. You need to think about longer-term investments.

You need a plan and a sensible long-term investment approach.

- The earlier you start the better.
- The smarter you invest the better.

Reason #2. To eliminate personal debt

Australians have a high level of personal debt, fuelled by relatively easy access to finance and the recent addition of buy-now pay-later products in many stores. You can have a new car, furniture, phone or IT equipment, but at a huge extra cost as credit cards can have very high costs and interest charges.

The problem is that this type of debt is really bad. The cost is usually high, while the asset behind the debt is depreciating fast. It makes no sense to have a high cost of debt when the asset ends up worth very little.

Based on Australian Bureau of Statistics (ABS) data, in 2015-16, 74 per cent of households held an average household debt of $168,600. The most common form of debt was credit card debt, held by 55 per cent of households, followed by home loans (34 per cent) and student loans (17 per cent).

Most store credit schemes and cards charge an interest rate of over 15 per cent per annum, and some as high as 20 per cent or more! If you are one of the 55 per cent with credit card debt in Australia, please read on.

To get yourself out of the credit trap, you need to learn to spend less and to invest.

Reason #3. To protect yourself from a rainy day event.

So, do you think that a major disaster such as an accident, your car being stolen, house going up in flames or being flooded, parents falling ill and needing care, a seriously sick child will never happen to you? And then there are external events: the global financial crisis and, more recently, the Coronavirus pandemic…

For many Australians Coronavirus is their first wake-up call — the realisation that events can occur we have no control over. And these events will change our outlook, future and sense of security drastically.

We have been lucky in Australia for generations as the general population has never really gone without since World War II, which ended in 1945. That was 75 years ago. And we haven't had a recession for 30 years. So, if you're 40 years old or younger, 2020 is your first ever recession.

Yes, there is poverty in this country and we have had recessions, but in general we are very well off.

There are many ways to measure Australia's relative wealth as a nation, one being median wealth per adult where Australia comes in at No. 2 in the world with $181,361.

Median and mean wealth per adult, in US dollars. Countries and subnational areas. Initially in rank order by median wealth. (2019 publication).[3]

Rank	Country or subnational area	Median wealth per adult ⇕ (US dollars)	Mean wealth per adult ⇕ (US dollars)	Adult population ⇕ (thousands)
1	Switzerland	227,891	564,653	6,866
2	Australia	181,361	386,058	18,655
3	Iceland	165,961	380,868	250
4	Hong Kong	146,887	489,258	6,267
5	Luxembourg	139,789	358,003	461

Source : Credit Suisse Global Wealth report

But, as we know, there may be tough periods in any economy or country.

So what is a rainy day event? A member of your family may fall ill, you may be injured or lose your job — the list goes on. Not many of us go through life unscathed — that's life. So you need to have a backup financial plan. And this plan should be to save some money, just in case.

According to a 2018 Australian study, 49 per cent of Australians old enough to save had saved less than $10,000. This is not enough to get through most issues.

A rule of thumb is to have at least three months' expenses in a rainy day account — and ideally six months and up to 12 months.

So how much is that?

For a single person paying a rent of $500 a week, running a car and a smartphone, and who likes going out, monthly expenses will be at least $5,000. So you should have at least $15,000 saved. Have you got that?

For a middle-aged couple with kids and a mortgage, this is more likely to be $30,000 - $50,000. If this is you, have you got that money?

And I like to suggest that a retiree should have one year of living costs in cash and 3-5 times that amount in defensive assets like bonds. So if you spend $50,000 a year, then you keep $50,000, just for peace of mind.

You need to know how to invest so you can survive a rainy day, month or year.

Reason #4. You will live a long time

Chances are you will live longer than your grandparents and your parents. Some people actually find this daunting, and often ask some of the following questions:

- How can I make sure I have enough money for that long?
- What if I live to 90, but want to retire at 60?
- What if I get sick and need expensive medical care?
- How can I make sure I have enough money to move into the aged-care facility I want or stay at home with personalised care?

Your working life is around 40 years, and you want to live off what you saved then for 30 years.

Most Australians can expect to live to at least 80, and if you are in your 20s now that will be more like 85.

THE SUPER SECRET

According to the Australian Institute of Health and Welfare, an Australian male born between 2014 and 2016 has a life expectancy of 80.4 years, and female life expectancy is 84.6 years, In fact, Australia now enjoys one of the highest life expectancies of any country in the world.

If you plan to work less when you reach 55, 60, 65 or 70, then you will be semi-retired or retired for a long time. If you're not investing wisely, you may not be able to work less or retire — you may have to keep on working if you can keep or find a job.

You simply have to invest to secure your long-term wealth and start to see the long-term picture. Unless of course you envisage living on the age pension, which in 2020 is about $430 per week.

Reason #5. To retire and be free

Leading straight on from reason #4 is the million-dollar question: how much will you need in retirement? Short answer: a lot. A slightly more nuanced answer is, as much money as you can possibly save.

The best way to have a great retirement is to start saving early. Ask anyone who is retired and they will tell you an 'if only' story — if only I had started saving a bit earlier, if only I had bought that property in 1982 that's now worth $3m.

If you can put away even small instalments during your 30s and 40s, then that will make a huge difference. It always seems expensive now. You never seem to have the money now. But it's this incremental saving that will help with your longer-term financial security.

It's time to take a long-term view and not have any regrets.

After all, your parents may live until 85 or more, so you can't bank on an early inheritance to get you through. Increasingly, they'll be using their savings and investments to fund their life, care and housing options.

The difference between starting when you are 30 or 40 to when you are 50 is huge. At 40 you probably have a lot of commitments, such as kids, sports, nice dinners and red wine. And it's hard to not dip into savings for a holiday, a new car or school fees.

But if you had $20,000 to invest at 40, and added $100 a month and invested it all in a low-cost diversified share fund, it could be worth over $325,000 by the time you are 65. And if you saved $200 a month, it could be worth $450,000 by the time you are 65.[3]

This is just simple maths and compound returns.

Long-term investing works. The earlier you start the better. The smarter you invest the better.

Superannuation is great, but most of us will need more than that. You have to invest to ensure that your future lifestyle is as good if not better than your current lifestyle.

You need to be a smart investor, because based on your life expectancy you will be retired for a long time. And require a lot of money.

How much will you need? Aim to have as much as you can. To do that means starting as early as you can.

---

3 The calculations used are based on various assumptions and should not be seen as a guarantee in returns or reflect your personal situation in any way. This is an illustration only of the effect of compound returns.

Reason #6. Superannuation

Australians have a great system called superannuation. It has some flaws, but in principle it's great. It is effectively tax-advantaged forced savings, and has raised the wealth of many Australians over what they would have achieved without this mandatory system. As a result, the whole nation is better off, because fewer people are relying on the age pension which we all have to cover through taxes.

However, many people still will not have enough money for their lifestyle in their superannuation.

To enhance your future lifestyle, you need to take some control of your superannuation to ensure it's well managed. After all, it is your money. You need to know what it's invested in, and to help steer the ship. Simply ignoring your superannuation until it's too late is not an option, and just putting it in a low-cost option is not good enough either. Costs are important, but what are you invested in?

The superannuation system actually allows you to invest the funds and have a lot of say, but the superfunds haven't told you that because they have a strong vested interest in making investing seem complicated as they make huge fees from investing your money.

You don't need to have a self-managed fund to make some smart decisions about your money.

Once you understand and want to invest in the philosophy and evidence-based approach I share with you in this book, you can invest this way in many superannuation accounts in Australia.

So why are almost three trillion dollars invested in expensive and underperforming funds?

Why is there 'lost super' – funds people have put in super accounts and never claimed?

Most people take very little interest in their superannuation, in fact only 35 per cent of Australians know how much money they have in superannuation![4]

You must change this: it is your money and it's too important to not take any interest and learn how to invest.

As of 30 June 2019, Australians had A$2.9 trillion in superannuation assets, making Australia the fourth largest holder of pension fund assets in the world.

You need to be a more knowledgeable investor to lead the pack and make sure your superannuation is successfully invested, but over time it will make a huge difference to your superannuation savings.

If you have $200,000 invested now in superannuation, a 2 percent difference in return over 20 years could make a difference of over $350,000 to your capital.[5] You have to know how this works.

Reason #7. To care for your children, parents-in-law and out-laws

Whether you have a family or not, plan to or not, there is a high chance that you are not the only person you worry about.

Most people have children or parents to care for. Mum and Dad may need to enter a care facility one day, so it's essential to understand how that works, and how to invest

---

4 Source https://financialcapability.gov.au/

5 Estimates are based on assumption-based compound growth rates and not intended to provide guarantees of future returns or outcomes.

their savings to pay for their care.

You may have a large family and need to save for education. You may get divorced and find yourself on your own, or part of a new, blended family.

Whatever your situation, your investments will need to make this all work out for you.

If looking after yourself and your family is important to you, you must learn how to invest properly.

Reason #8. To be independent from the government
I don't believe any financial advice should include relying on the government. We should all plan to be completely financially independent. And most of us can be if we know how to invest.

Government is there as a backstop for those who need it, and that is awesome. Australia has a pretty good system. It's not perfect, but try living in any other country and Australia comes out pretty well. We have lots of opportunities, but we also look after our sick, incapable, disabled, elderly and those in need. The system also helps many people who would not need government funding if they had understood how to invest sooner.

If more Australians invest earlier then they will not need government help unless there is an emergency. And this means there is more money available to look after people who really need help.

For example, if every Australian invested $1,000 at birth in a share fund that earned 8 per cent a year compound over 60 years, how much would they have at 60?

The answer is just over $93,000.

Now let's change that initial amount invested to $2,000. The result is just over $187,000

And how about $5,000 – it would be $468,000.[6]

This is without any tricky investment management or even adding funds.

Long-term investing works, and the earlier you start the better. It is that simple.

We should all plan to be self-sufficient and only rely on the government when really necessary. If you know how to invest, you will not ever have to rely on government support.

Reason #9. Australia is a growing country. This means opportunity.

We have a growing population, plenty of space, intelligent people and lots of opportunities.

According to the Australian Bureau of Statistics (ABS) the Australian population is now 26 million and forecast to be 30 million by 2030 and 40 million by 2050.

We are a fortunate country, and with a rising population come more growth and opportunity. There is plenty of land, and progress will provide more employment and business opportunities. We should think big and, for example, build larger inland cities and better infrastructure.

Here is an example of forward planning and thinking big: the Sydney Harbour Bridge was planned in the 1920s and completed in 1932. It has six lanes, train lanes, and

---

6 The projections here use various assumptions that do not try to predict or guarantee future returns or take into account your personal circumstances, but illustrate the benefits of investing for longer periods of time and the compound returns.

used to have tram lanes. It connects on the northern side to the Warringah Expressway, which was intended to go all the way to Warringah, 10 km north of the city, but it ends in Cammeray which is only a few hundred metres to the north. In 1932 an average of 10,000 cars crossed the bridge every day. Why do we not build motorways with 10 lanes today, and why are we still debating roads like the Spit Bridge and tunnels to Warringah in 2021 when town planners in the 1920s were thinking like that?

We need to think bigger as a nation, and this is just one example. I'd like to see a plan for an inland city, like Las Vegas in the US. I'm not a gambler and I don't go to casinos except for events or conferences but, for gamblers and tourists, rather than building more casinos in Sydney, Melbourne and Brisbane, why not make Broken Hill our Las Vegas? That would create boundless jobs and opportunities. But that's for another book!

Australians need to think big and invest for the long term.

And as an investor you need to be part of this growth.[7]

Reason #10. To pass wealth on to the next generation.

If you invest successfully, you will not spend all your money. How nice to set up a legacy for the next generation and beyond, especially when today's under-25s are entering a radically different economic environment to ours: constant

---

7 Australia's Federal Government has announced generational infrastructure projects in June 2020 to reboot the economy in response to the coronavirus. This is a positive start to bring the states together, reduce red tape and build for the future.

gig work, large HECS debt, fewer jobs, increasing taxes, unaffordable housing.

There is going to be a huge transfer of wealth over the next 30 years as baby boomers[8] pass their super and assets on to the next generations. If you are doing this, or are likely to receive these assets, do you know how to invest?

Your kids or grandkids may have large sums of money to manage. Don't you want to make sure they are well-informed and have sound investment skills?

If you are not an investor now but suddenly inherit some funds, will you be comfortable with the responsibility? For many people, money is actually a problem and creates anxiety. Why? Because they worry about the daily news and which stocks to pick, attend seminars about buying options, property and bitcoin and other get-rich-quick ideas. Imagine not having to worry about all that and investing successfully without the stress and anxiety?

If you know how to invest successfully, you won't have to worry about your investments and can devote yourself to doing what you like.

There are many other reasons why it's important to be a smart investor, but these 10 demonstrate why you should create a plan and accept that you need to know more about investing and the truth behind it.

---

8 Individuals born after World War II, between 1946 and 1964.

CHAPTER 2 SUMMARY

» Every one of us is an investor or will be, so we owe it to ourselves and our families to understand how to invest successfully.

» Learning about the fundamentals and principles of investing that put you the investor first, could make the difference between a lousy retirement and an amazing retirement.

» Sharing this knowledge with your children, grandchildren and family can help them avoid mistakes that many make , and save them thousands over their lifetime.

3

It's Time To Change The Way You Think About Investing
Something has been going on in global markets for a long time, and it's high time you knew about it

"The important thing is to not stop questioning. Curiosity has its own reason for existing." Albert Einstein

We are all investors, and it's important to become a better investor.

You are investing for various reasons that are important to you, so you need the best information to invest soundly and not get led into poor decisions, products or schemes.

The behaviours or habits that lead to success in all aspects of life have similar themes, and investing should be no different. To be successful in business, sport, music, investing or whatever you do typically requires:

- Time and commitment
- A great process
- Discipline

- Research
- Implementation
- Engagement with others, or a community of similar people
- Continual learning from the best
- Coaching or accountability
- Measurement.

Many investors follow no proper process for success. Common investment strategies are to do nothing, use lots of different approaches, chop and change daily or weekly, give your money to a bank, trade with a broker, buy into 'hot tips', or just guess. Many investors simply hand money over to someone else or an institution based on one advertisement they saw on the back of a bus that promises low costs, higher returns, guaranteed returns or just the image of a lifestyle.

Many others do try hard by themselves, but with very little success. I have met so many investors over the years who pick their own stocks, but they have no idea how they have performed in the past. They simply don't know. Studies measuring individual stock-picking performance indicate that they rarely perform over time. This is logical, given that global managers with very smart teams and sophisticated technology struggle to beat market benchmarks, so it is unlikely someone trading on their own from home will have a better chance of success. The chart below shows research from Dalbar.com. The research suggests that individuals tend to perform a lot worse than the market.

Individuals fail to achieve market returns.

Annualised Returns
(for the 20 year period ending December 31, 2019)

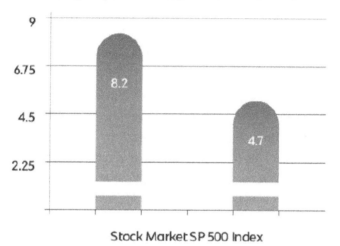

Stock Market S P 500 Index

Source: "DALBAR's 22nd Annual Quantitative Analysis of Investor Behavior." DALBAR, Inc. 2016
Indexes are not available for direct investment. Their performance does not reflect the expenses
associated with the management of an actual portfolio. Past performance is not a guarantee of
future results.

This is not their fault, many parts of the investment industry actually want you to behave in this way.

In the film *The Wolf of Wall Street*, brokers' behaviour was explained by Mark Hanna, played by Matthew McConaughey, to new recruit Jordan Belfort, played by Leonardo Di Caprio. When Jordan says he is excited to be joining the firm and working for clients, Mark quickly tells him how the "game" works, and how it's not about the client at all:

Mark Hanna:

The name of the game, moving the money from the clients pocket to your pocket.

Jordan

But if you can make your clients money at the same time it's advantageous to everyone, correct?

Mark Hanna:

No.

Mark Hanna:

The No. 1 rule of Wall Street is: "Nobody, I don't care if you are Warren Buffet... Nobody knows if the stock is going to go up, down, sideways or in circles! Least of all stockbrokers!"

You should not feel too bad about this story or the data if you have managed money, have been trying to find the latest stock to buy, purchased investor magazines or followed broker research – because the broking model is not about you at all.

It may alarm or intrigue you to know that even professional investment managers find it really hard to outperform.

Many investment managers attempt to outperform the market by taking advantage of so-called mispricing opportunities. They use research, insights and intuition to predict which securities will perform better in the future. Now many investment managers are intelligent and have very large teams and sophisticated systems and models, so you would expect that they could outperform on a regular, consistent basis.

However, decades of data and evidence show that for an active manager to consistently and over long periods identify in advance the few stocks that account for much of the market return each year is very difficult.

In fact, the odds of success are very slim and the out-performers random. Research papers have shown that outperforming funds seldom continue to outperform.[9]

Very few have consistently beaten the market — so few that it's not a risk worth taking for most investors.

There are many reasons for this. One is that a few stocks' strong performance accounts for much of the market's return each year. This makes picking stocks difficult, because the odds are weighted against you.

Markets are pretty good at disseminating all available information and putting it in the price of a stock. It's very hard to have information no one else has day after day.

And there are fund management and trading costs.

Also, many managers don't stand the test of time, as shown in the image overleaf.[10]

---

9 Mutual Fund Landscape Report 2020 Dimensional Fund Advisors
10 Chart sourced from Mutual Fund Landscape Report 2020 Dimensional Fund Advisors

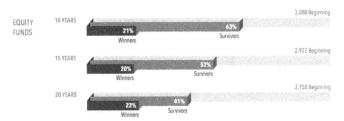

Few US-Domiciled Mutual Funds Have Survived and Outperformed
Performance periods ending December 31, 2019

Other reasons will be shown later in the book, but the evidence and facts are publicly available and compelling.

I am not suggesting these managers are incompetent. They are highly intelligent and ethical, doing the best they can. It's just how markets work and what the data has shown us over many, many years.

According to data from Standard and Poor's[11], for the five-year period to December 31 2019, 80.79 per cent of Australian funds underperformed the broader market index.

---

11 For more information go to the Standard and Poor's site https://au.spindices.com/spiva/#/

AUSTRALIA

PERCENTAGE OF AUSTRALIAN EQUITY GENERAL FUNDS THAT
UNDERPERFORMED THE S&P/ASX 200

Data as of Dec 31, 2019

FIVE-YEAR

80.79%

THREE-YEAR

74.54%

ONE-YEAR

61.52%

GET STATS FOR OTHER MARKET SEGMENTS >

PERSISTENCE
DOES PAST PERFORMANCE REALLY MATTER?
THE PERSISTENCE SCORECARD TRACKS THE STAYING POWER OF TOP ACTIVE PERFORMERS OVER TIME.

Chart sourced from https://us.spindices.com/spiva/#/

Have you ever heard the saying "You don't know what you don't know"?

Did you know that billions of dollars have been leaving conventional managed funds for low-cost, evidence-based and index funds for many years now? How come we don't know about this in Australia?

It's official: inexpensive index funds have finally eclipsed old-fashioned stock pickers. Passive investing styles have been gaining ground on actively managed funds for decades. But in August the investment industry reached one of the biggest milestones in modern history as assets in U.S. index-based equity mutual funds and ETFs topped those in active stock funds for the first time.[12]

To invest successfully, we have to leave our ego at the door, forget our past mistakes and open our minds to a better way to invest.

Over the years I have seen many people invest in a certain way simply because that is all they know, and they do not look for what they don't know. Many also, despite the evidence that their investments have not worked, hang on due to ego and other psychological reasons.

I want to reiterate that there is a logical and rational explanation for most individuals and professional managers not outperforming, and there is a way to invest successfully without a crystal ball, picking stocks or a guru fund manager.

What is an index fund?

An index fund is a type of managed investment fund with a portfolio constructed to match or track the components of a financial market index, such as the Standard & Poor's 500 Index (S&P 500) which is the largest 500 companies on the American market, or ASX 200 which is the largest 200 companies on the Australian market. An index fund is said to provide broad market exposure, low operating expenses and low portfolio turnover. Index funds are also commonly referred to as passive funds.

---

12 Bloomberg.com September 12, 2019: Asset Managers With $74 Trillion on Brink of Historic Shakeout, Suzy Waite, Annie Massa and Christopher Cannon. Author John Gittelsohn

What is an ETF?

An exchange-traded managed fund is simply a managed fund that is traded on a stock exchange.

What is a managed fund?

A managed fund is a pool of lots of investments into one trust. For example, an Australian share index fund will hold 200 shares in one investment so instead of having to go out and buy all 200 shares, you can simply buy units in the fund.

What is an active fund?

In the investment industry, actively managed funds are managed by investment managers who trade a lot to try and outperform the market, i.e. they actively stock pick or attempt to use forecasts and time the market.

Now you have some insight into the data, don't you agree it's time to change the way you think about investing?

CHAPTER 3 SUMMARY

» You now know there is a different way to invest.
» You now have access to research to show that the conventional way of investing has a low probability of success: some investments will outperform, but most won't.

4

The Super Secret - Introducing Evidence-Based Investing

What is evidence-based investing?

"Evidence-based investing is using the findings (evidence) from the leading minds in finance to learn about how invest-ment markets really work and to implement those ideas into portfolios." Robin Powell, TheEvidencebasedinvestor.com

"Once you accept this view of markets, the benefits go way beyond just investing money." David Booth, Founder, Dimensional Fund Advisors with $739bn AUD under man-agement across 13 global offices

Now that we have looked at the industry as end investors, and seen that conventional investing has a lower chance of success than we were told, we can either give up and not trust the industry at all or look for a solution. The point is that markets do provide returns, so all we need to do is find the best way to capture them.

Decades of data show that a conventional stock picking and market timing approach to managing money has not been successful in the past. The odds of success are very low. Some managers will win, but most will lose. How do you know in advance which manager will win? The only answer to that is luck.

Managing your own funds through an online broker account shows no evidence of success, sustainability or governance. If the professionals can't do it with all their teams and analysis, how can you possibly outperform with your home internet and online trading account? It just makes no sense.

Fortunately, there is a better way.

For over 70 years economists studied and tried to explain why most investment managers struggle to outperform.

However the world of finance has worked out that you do not need to rely on forecasts or market timing, or implement high trading or stock picking strategies to have a successful investment outcome.

The findings from academia about how to invest, peer-reviewed for decades, are remarkably consistent and well-entrenched.

Evidence-based investing flips the traditional invest-ment model and uses:

- Science rather than guesswork to guide investment decisions
- Structure and process rather than hype to frame your allocation.

Evidence-based investing consults the smartest minds in finance, who have no objective other than to uncover the truth, as opposed to salespeople who have been shown to have absolutely no reason to put your interests first.

There is no hidden fee or commission or free ticket to cricket or footy this weekend in evidence-based investing.

If you have not heard about evidence-based investing before, that is because there is no commission in it for banks or planners. The only way you would know about it is by having engaged an independent fee only adviser or sheer luck.

Most investment professionals and industry commentators are either unaware of evidence-based investing, ignore it, or try to hide it from you for their own reasons, although it is widely recognised in academic circles.

By following an educated, evidence-based investment strategy, you are more likely to:

- Know that your interests come first
- Have a better chance of investment success
- Ensure that your investments will be around for a long time
- Maximise returns
- Stress less about investment markets
- Reach your lifestyle goals
- Manage emotions better and not make common behavioural mistakes.

There are a number of great books on how to manage your day-to-day finances better, including Scott Pape's *The Barefoot Investor* which I highly recommend. It's a brilliant book.

But Scott's book and the others don't cover the smarter way to invest your money. While there are thousands of books and websites telling you how to invest, most of them leave you with no clear strategy or, even worse, tell you to try and pick stocks. Even Scott's book does not refer to an evidence-based investing approach. No Australian investment books do.

In fact, most investment books leave you even more confused, or pitch a complicated trading methodology that is impossible to replicate in real life.

The main reason for this is that the old model of advice in Australia usually puts the product first and the client last. I want to make sure that every time you invest, the client – you – comes first. Until recently, there were very few independent advisers in Australia.

CHAPTER 4 SUMMARY

» Evidence-based investing has been around for a long time.
» Academics have shown us over many decades that there is a smarter way to invest.
» The world of finance has worked out that you do not need to rely on forecasts or market timing, or implement high trading or stock picking strategies to have a successful investment outcome.

5

The Key Principles of Evidence-Based Investing

"Ideas alone are cheap - implementation is what really counts" Myron Scholes

There are six principles in the framework that give the best chance of investment success using an evidence-based approach:

1. The investor or client always comes first
2. A belief in capital markets
3. Risk and reward are related
4. Diversification reduces investment risk
5. Asset allocation is important as it goes a long way to determining performance
6. Maintaining discipline via rebalancing.

Principle 1. The investor or client always comes first
A Leap Of Faith

I am confident that the investment industry can produce a fundamental shift in focus and put clients first.

So, if you are willing to take that leap of faith with me,

get ready to outstrip everything you think or have been told about how markets work: take control of your own investments and improve your future.

Principle 2. A belief in capital markets

As an investor, you get a premium for investing money out of cash into shares, property and riskier assets. This is capitalism working for you. It's a simple model really: if you take risk you need an opportunity for reward. So first of all there has to be belief in capital markets. Probably the only countries today that don't trust capital markets are North Korea and Cuba.

This principle is fundamental to evidence-based investing. We are investing in a capitalist model and need to believe that market pricing works efficiently, that it is a mechanism to determine a price, and these prices contain all information available at any given time and are inherently accurate.

Of course this belief translates to everything we do, whether buying furniture, petrol and groceries or shares, property and bonds.

Prices are not always perfect, but we are better off investing believing that capitalism works rather than the alternative where markets are not free to operate.

Principle 3. Risk and reward are related

The next step is to understand that risk and reward are related. The expected rate of return is a good indicator of the risk involved.

To understand capital markets and risk, it is important

to know what an asset class is and the various classes, because different asset classes have different risks and different expected returns.

Asset classes can be defined in very broad terms, such as equity or fixed income.

They can also be defined through specific categories, such as small cap stock or large cap growth stock. The asset class holds all securities that satisfy the asset class definition irrespective of fund manager's opinions about the future performance of individual stocks or sectors. We use asset classes as the building blocks of our asset allocation strategy because each class represents different risk/reward characteristics that can be combined into a truly diversified portfolio.

Even during times of great economic turmoil, many asset classes will have positive returns. A crisis of some kind may result in some or many equity asset classes turning negative, but how do you know which ones? For how long? This appears to be random. That is the point of efficient markets and why active management does not work.

Combining the risk/return characteristics of multiple asset classes in on portfolio serves to optimise returns and lower overall risk. This disciplined asset allocation program is a prudent way to manage your investments in volatile markets.

What is asset allocation?

Asset Allocation means spreading your investments across various asset classes. Broadly speaking, that is a mix of shares, property bonds, and cash or money market securities. Within these asset classes there are subclasses:

- Large-cap shares: Shares issued by companies with a market capitalisation of above $10 billion (global market).
- Mid-cap shares: Shares issued by companies with a market capitalisation of between $2 billion and $10 billion.
- Small-cap shares: Companies with a market capitalisation of less than $2 billion. These equities tend to have a higher risk due to their lower liquidity.
- International securities: Any security issued by a foreign company and listed on a foreign exchange.

- Emerging markets: Securities issued by companies in developing nations. These investments offer a high potential return and a high risk, due to possible country risk and their lower liquidity.
- Fixed income securities (also called fixed interest and bonds): Highly rated corporate or government bonds that pay the holder a set amount of interest periodically or at maturity, and return the principal at the end of the period. These securities are less volatile and less risky than stocks.
- Money market: Investments in short-term debt, typically a year or less. Treasury bills (T-bills) are the most common money market investment.
- Real estate investment trusts (REITs): Shares in an investor pool of mortgaged properties.

Evidence from decades of data, investor experience and academics point to one undeniable conclusion: returns come from risk. The higher the return, the higher the risk.

When you hear an advertisement on the radio for a "low risk, cash fund that is generating 6 per cent" but the cash rate is only 0.5 per cent, then this 'investment' is a lot riskier than cash and probably not that safe. This may seem obvious, but these advertised products lure billions of dollars from investors every year.

The basic questions for would-be investors are:

- How do I make sure I am rewarded for taking risks?
- Where is the best place to invest to ensure my risk is rewarded?

- How do I ensure my assets that should not be risky are in fact low risk?

Not all risks carry a reliable reward. It is important we capture returns and understand risk to have a successful investment experience.

In equity markets everything we have learned about expected returns can be summarised in four statements:

1. Shares are riskier, but have higher expected returns than bonds.
2. The size of a company: small companies are riskier and have higher expected returns than large companies. This makes sense because small companies have a higher cost of capital, which may grow faster, but may also fail.
3. The price of a company's shares: lower priced 'value' stocks are riskier and offer higher expected returns than higher priced 'growth' stocks. A value stock is one whose price has dropped for one reason or another.
4. The profitability of a company: profitable companies have higher expected returns than lower profit companies.

Fixed Interest and bonds compared to shares

This diagram explains the difference to the end investor between bonds and shares. They are both mechanisms for a company to raise money or capital. As an investor in shares you receive a return for that share in ownership, while a bond investor is really lending money so receives interest.

Stocks and Bonds are Conduits for Capital

Stocks and Bonds Are Conduits for Capital

So what is a bond?

A bond is a loan from you to a government or company. You receive interest, often called a coupon, and the rate or yield is the income you receive. It's also a reflection of the risk. For example, in the current climate a government bond may be offering 3 per cent versus a small company offering 8 per cent.

Clearly in this case lending to a small company is riskier than lending your money to a government.

While bonds have exhibited good long-term returns, many investors shy away from them and either invest in cash or riskier alternatives because they believe the rate of return is too low, the time is not right or that interest rates will go up.

Bonds may be used for many reasons, and here are four good ones:

1. To earn a better rate than cash
2. To preserve capital
3. To provide liquidity
4. To provide diversification.

With bonds, risk comes from two particular dimensions:

1. Term - the length of the bond: the longer the bond or 'loan' the riskier it is. For example, a short-term government bond is riskier than cash, but not as risky as a long-term corporate bond.

2. Credit - the rating given to a bond issue: For example, the Australian government has a higher credit rating than a small company issuing a bond and is therefore safer, but will have a lower return.

Holding a diversified portfolio of global bonds of mixed credit and duration is another important element of a successful long-term portfolio.

There is an inverse relationship between the price and yield of a bond. In other words, when the price goes up the yield typically diminishes, and when the price of a bond falls the yield increases.

In this diagram the dimensions of return are explained for equities and fixed interest.

Dimensions of Expected Returns

EQUITIES

Company Size (Market Capitalisation)

Relative Price (Price/Book Equity)

Profitability (Operating Profits/Book Equity)

FIXED INTEREST

Term (Sensitive to Interest Rates)

Credit (Credit Quality of Issuer)

Currency (Currency of Issuance)

There is a wealth of academic research into what drives returns. Expected returns depend on current market prices and expected future cash flows. Investors can use this information to pursue higher expected returns in their portfolios.

Relative price is measured by the price-to-book ratio; value stocks are those with lower price-to-book ratios. Profitability is measured as operating income before depreciation and amortisation minus interest expense scaled by book.

Source for diagram Dimensional fund advisors

The pivotal dimensions of share markets

The market
Shares have a higher expected return than bonds or cash. They don't always perform better, but over time they have in the past, and this would be expected to continue in a capitalist system.

The size of the company
Large companies have different expected returns to small companies. If I am running a small company, I have a higher cost of capital to raise funds and grow my company. This increases my risk, but if it pays off my small company can grow faster than a large company.

So should I only hold small companies? No, there is risk involved. While small companies have a higher expected return, they also have a higher risk, but having some small companies in a portfolio in a diversified approach can help increase returns.

More conservative investors may wish to just hold larger companies that have a lower expected return than smaller companies and are less risky.

The price of the company
The share price of a listed company tells us a lot. If the company's share price drops, it may be for many reasons – an event out of the company's control like the coronavirus, bad management, government policy, structural changes in the sector, fraud, illegal activities, a major environmental/ social disaster or a combination of these.

If the price drops significantly then it might be judged good value, of course, but how low will it go? Can the company recover?

A parcel of value companies has a higher expected return than a parcel of companies with high share prices. This can be seen in many instances, not just in share markets. In essence, there is a return to normal just like in sports where, on average, most teams revert when they drop to the bottom of the table — not all, but most.

However if you try to pick one value company only it can be dangerous. That company may be going out of business. It may never win again.

The value premium can be seen over time and over many markets, but might also not show up for many years, so you need to be patient.

Historical premiums and returns (annualised)

- Academic research has identified groups of securities that have delivered higher returns (or premiums) over time
- These premiums may be positive or negative in any given year
- Over longer periods, historically the expectation of positive premiums increases
- Investing in portfolios that target multiple premiums helps increase the reliability of outcomes

Source Dimensional fund advisors

The profitability of a company

Research has also shown that firms with higher profitability tend to have higher returns than those with low profitability. This is referred to as a profitability premium.

This study was initially carried out by Robert Novy Marx, while at about the same time the research team at Dimensional was also analysing profitability. They extended the work of Fama and French and found that in developed and emerging markets globally, current profitability can teach us about future profitability, and that firms with higher profitability have had higher returns than those with low profitability. This observation holds true when using different measures of current profitability. These robustness checks are important to show that the profitability premiums observed in the original studies were not just due to chance.

So if you only buy large companies and diversify, you will most likely do better over time than stock pickers, mainly due to lower costs (you don't charge yourself management fees), lower capital gains taxes and survivorship — the very fact that your investment manager exists 10 years later is called survivorship.

To enhance returns, you can tilt your portfolio to different factors or dimensions like value and small companies to increase your return, but remember there is no return without risk.

Capital Markets Have Rewarded
Long-Term Investors

Monthly growth of wealth ($1), October 1989 – December 2019

In Australian dollars. Australian inflation rate provided by the Australian Bureau of Statistics. Data provided by Bloomberg Finance L.P. S&P/ASX data copyright 2020 S&P Dow Jones Indices LLC, a division of S&P Global. All rights reserved. Indices are not available for direct investment. Their performance does not reflect the expenses associated with the management of an actual portfolio. Past performance not indicative of future performance.

Property

There are two basic types of investment in property: your home and investment property.

Your home is an asset and based on different fundamentals to an investment decision. Try not to change homes too often; the transfer costs of stamp duty, agent commissions, marketing and removal are very high.

In Australia your home is capital gains tax free and usually an asset you will leave to family. In addition, it gives you both emotional and financial security.

Property investment, just like shares, is based on looking for a return on your capital as in the increase in the price of the property over time, and provides income in the form of rent.

You can invest in property directly by buying a residential unit, house or commercial property.

You can also buy property through a trust that owns lots of properties. Different property trusts specialise in different property types: commercial, industrial, residential.

Property is a great asset, but comes with risks just like any other asset.

A commercial property has a higher risk of the tenant leaving, and being vacant for longer periods of time. Just think of all the commercial tenants that have had to close down their businesses due to the coronavirus and the rent freezes required by law or necessity. A number of those will not reopen.

The critical investment decision you make in relation to property will be based on:

- Your time frame (how long you plan to hold the property for)
- Liquidity
- Tax outcomes
- Borrowing costs.

The evolution of dimensions;
These factors or dimensions have evolved from academic research dating back to 1963 with a single factor to 2012, and profitability being added.

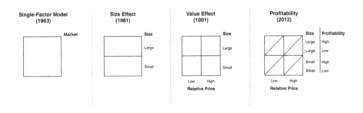

In this diagram we see the four fundamental dimensions of returns and the criteria for a dimension to be applied.

Dimensions of Expected Returns

Expected returns are driven by prices investors pay and cash flows they expect to receive

To be considered a dimension of expected return, a premium must be:

- Sensible
- Persistent
- Pervasive
- Robust
- Cost-effective

The benefits of investing in small companies and value companies can be seen for long periods in all markets. Risk is rewarded.

Dimensions of Expected Returns

Historical premiums and returns (annualised)

Australia Stocks

Company Size
Relative performance of small cap stocks vs. large cap stocks (%)

1974–2019

1.91

13.78 11.87

Small minus Large | Small | Large

Annualised Returns

Relative Price
Relative performance of value stocks vs. growth stocks (%)

1975–2019

5.49

15.76 10.27

Value minus Growth | Value | Growth

Annualised Returns

Profitability
Relative performance of high profitability stocks vs. low profitability stocks (%)

1983–2019

5.31

13.21 7.90

High Prof. minus Low Prof. | High Prof. | Low Prof.

Annualised Returns

The data also shows that these premiums exist in US stocks and markets and emerging markets. There is a clear premium increase in value and small companies. This is illustrated below:

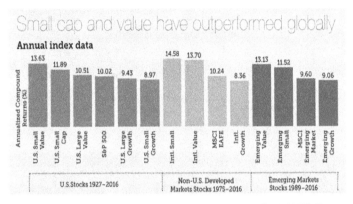

Source of charts Dimensional Fund Advisors

This chart shows the risk frontier - as the expected return increases so does the standard deviation which is a mathematical calculation for risk. The S&P 500 is the broad index of US shares, which are riskier than Treasury bills issued by the government. As your risk or standard deviation increases, so does your expected return.

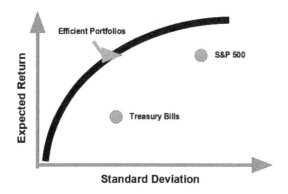

This choice between whether you invest in cash or shares or property is very important, and will have a real impact on your long-term return.

Principle 4. Diversification reduces risk

The first way to reduce risk is to diversify using your asset allocation. How much is invested in shares, cash, bonds or property will determine your risk and return.

While cash is the less risky investment, not investing means taking risks too. In 1918, 14 cents was enough to buy a container of milk whereas today in Australia a 2-litre milk carton costs between $2 and $4. So it's a logical step that if you do not invest your cash it will not be able to buy as much in the future. Investing ensures that your assets grow at least in line with inflation and, hopefully, by more to improve your wealth and purchasing power.

Your Money Today Will Likely
Buy Less Tomorrow

1919	1969	2019
$0.16 = Quart of milk	$0.16 = 2 Cups of milk	$0.16 = 12 Tablespoons of milk

In US dollars.
Source for 1919 and 1969: Historical Statistics of the United States, Colonial Times to 1970/US Department of Commerce. Source for 2019: US Department of Labor, Bureau of Labor Statistics, Economic Statistics, Consumer Price Index – US City Average Price Data.

It is important to diversify or spread your investments so that you don't just hold cash, but also invest in shares, bonds, property and other assets.

Holding securities across many market segments can help manage overall risk. Many investors think of their own market as the only market to invest in.

But diversifying within your home market may not be enough. Global diversification should broaden your investment universe, and help capture as well as smooth out returns.

Diversification does not eliminate negative returns, but can improve your long-term performance as a more consistent portfolio will perform better than a volatile portfolio. Within these asset classes it is important to invest where there is evidence of relative performance for the risk taken. In other words, there is no point investing in an asset if it is risky but has a low rate of return.

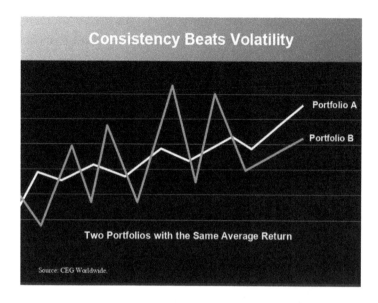

It is important when you invest in an asset class that you actually achieve the return that capital markets deliver over time. In other words, if you invest in Australian shares and go to Antarctica for the next 20 years and never look at markets for that entire time, whether you like it or not you will get a return on your money. Let's say that return is 10 per cent per annum over the whole period. What you don't want to happen is to return and find out even though the market delivered 10 per cent, you only had a 6 per cent return due to costs or poor investments. The fact is, the market drives most of your return.

It's also important to consider global portfolios to diversify, invest in different industries and reduce exposure to small or concentrated markets. Some markets may have prolonged flat periods or periods of outperformance.

By looking to overseas investments, you greatly increase your opportunity to invest in superior global firms that can help you grow your wealth.

Global diversification in your portfolio also reduces its overall risk. The price movements between international asset classes are often dissimilar, so investing globally can increase your portfolio's diversification.

Home Market
Index Portfolio

S&P/ASX 300 Index
1 country,
296 stocks

Global Market
Index Portfolio

MSCI ACWI
Investable
Market Index (IMI)
49 countries,
9,031 stocks

Holding securities across many
market segments can help
manage overall risk. But
diversifying within your home
market may not be enough.
Global diversification can
broaden your
investment universe.

When we look at risk, it can be broken down into segments or dimensions of the market.

Different types of shares have different levels of risk:

- Shares are riskier than bonds. However they offer higher expected returns as a reward.
- Small companies have higher expected returns than large companies. This makes sense because small companies have a higher cost of capital and, by definition, could grow faster, but also may fail.
- Lower priced 'value' stocks offer higher expected returns than higher-priced 'growth' stocks.
- A value stock is one whose price has dropped for one reason or another.
- Profitable companies have higher expected returns than lower profit companies.

No one knows with any certainty which market or sector will be the best next year, or even next month — possibly even tomorrow. As a result, it is important to have a globally diversified portfolio and also ensure effective diversification. Value and small sectors have certainly performed well over time, but this comes with increased risk. There are also periods when these segments or dimensions of the market do not outperform. If we look at market performance over time, as shown in the image below, there is no real pattern or any way to reliably predict which market will perform next in each year. Can you see a pattern?

Periodic Table of Assets—AUD
January 2003–December 2019

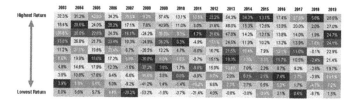

Source of charts Dimensional Fund Advisors

Eugene Fama and Kenneth French, both highly respected academics, developed the three–factor model.

Fama and French started by looking at the size of companies and how much a stock's price was above or below its accounting book value and then used this information to divide the market into categories. They took half of the companies, those with the largest market value, and placed them into the large cap category, and the other half was placed in the small cap category. Next, if the company's stock price was relatively high compared to its book value, it was placed in the growth category, and if the stock price was relatively low compared to its book value, it was placed in the value category. They made no attempt to evaluate good or bad companies, or good or bad management. The average annual return of the large cap growth companies is 9.47% and for large cap value companies it is 10.28%. The difference between those two annual rates of return is 0.81%. Similarly, the annual return in small cap growth companies is 9.03% and 13.35% for small cap value: a difference of 4.32%

– 55 –

But you can't afford to take bets and stay out of a certain market or only invest in certain markets.

Diversification is ensuring you capture asset classes effectively and efficiently.

I have seen many different Australian share fund managers' portfolios over the years, and just about all of them hold the same shares. Is that diversification? No.

You can achieve the same exposure or better with one investment manager more efficiently than having 20 different fund managers' names in your report . The risk is in the underlying shares, so it's important to have more shares and not necessarily more managers.

Once you understand how to diversify and what you are diversifying, you realise that the risk is the under-lying shares you own. Actually, having more investment managers stock picking or market timing increases your risk and defeats the whole purpose of diversifying.

Principle 5. Asset allocation is important as it goes a long way to determining performance

What is the biggest contributor to portfolio performance? Asset allocation or stock selection?

The biggest decision is which asset allocation to be in, not which stock. The impact of the asset allocation far outweighs the impact of an individual stock over the long term. This is illustrated in the Asset Allocation is Key chart below.

You no longer have to buy the latest investment magazine telling you which six stocks to buy. Firstly because they don't really know, and secondly even if they did it is unlikely to make a significant difference to your long-term performance.

So even if you did know or had a broker who sells you the idea that BHP is better than Rio Tinto today — it doesn't really matter over the long term. That in itself is a game-breaker for many investors. You just don't have to worry about this type of activity.

And the fact that I don't know with any certainty whether BHP or RIO will be a better investment over the next 10 years, and no one does, will not actually have any impact on your future goals. What a revelation and how refreshing to hear! Research shows that asset allocation contributes over 90 per cent of your portfolio return, stock selection around 4 per cent and market timing only 2 per cent.

The good news is you can control your asset allocation.

Therefore if we focus on what we can control, rather than investing using a method that relies on factors we can't control, then we have a far greater chance of success.

Asset Allocation is Key

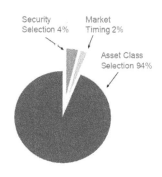

Asset Class Selection
How assets are allocated in a portfolio

Market Timing
Shifting portfolio assets in and out of the market or between asset classes.

Security Selection
Finding "underpriced" companies or industries.

Security Selection 4%   Market Timing 2%

Asset Class Selection 94%

The vast majority of a portfolio's returns variance is determined by asset class selection and only a small portion is determined by market timing and security selection.*

*Source: Study of 91 large pension plans over 10 year period.
Gary P. Brinson, L. Randolph Hood and Gilbert L. Beebower, "Determinants of Portfolio Performance", Financial Analysts Journal, July-August 1986, pp. 39-44;
and Gary P. Brinson, Brian D. Singer and Gilbert L. Beebower, "Revisiting Determinants of Portfolio Performance: An Update", 1990, Working Paper.

Generally speaking, the more time you have the more money you may wish to have invested in long-term assets like shares and property.

Markets have rewarded long-term investors and I can't see any reason why this will not continue.

You have to believe in markets and take an optimistic view of the future. There have been world wars, plagues, famines, market collapses, massive bush fires, earthquakes, tsunamis and pandemics in the past 100 years. Yet investors have still been rewarded.

In his book *Abundance*, Peter Diamandis explains that the evolution of technology, health and pace of development should lead to better lives for everyone. According to the World Bank, the number of people living on less than $1 day has more than halved since the 1950s to below 18 percent of the population. This number is in itself almost too huge to comprehend, but shows that the pace of change is faster than ever before.[13]

Even in cities like Sydney, as recently as the 1960s many houses were not on a septic or sewage system and sewage was collected weekly, which is why there were always laneways for the night cart. The developed world has achieved unimaginable improvements over the past 50 years. For example, look at how fast technology has changed our lives. When do you think the first iPhone was sold? June 29 2007! 2.2 billion have now been sold and here is a picture of the first model:

13 Quotes from Abundance, by Peter Diamandis, which also refers to The Rational Optimist by Matt Ridley.

How do people invest to increase their wealth? Most look to the financial markets as their main investment avenue.

The good news is that the capital markets have rewarded long-term investors. There's an expected return to free-market capitalism — and historically the markets have provided a long-term return that has offset inflation.

It's important to keep in mind that there's risk and uncertainty in the markets and that past results may not be repeated in the future. Investors demand a positive expected return. Otherwise, they wouldn't invest.

So while it is important to invest in riskier assets like shares and property and to believe that future market returns will be similar to or better than the past, you also want to ensure you have enough cash and bonds. Why?

There are three main reasons for having safer assets.

1. Liquidity and access to cash for income or a rainy day event
2. To protect and diversify your portfolio in the event of short-term volatility. Growth markets can have sudden swings like in 2010, and sustained periods of lower returns like 2008/2009. The second chart below titled Bonds as a Buffer illustrates this point:
3. For income generation: bonds have been good income investments over time.

This chart shows how over time shares and bonds have rewarded long term investors

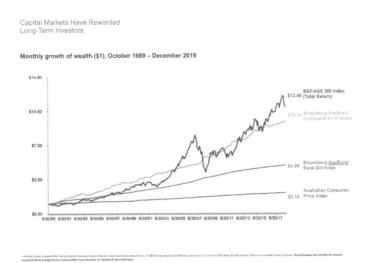

Capital Markets Have Rewarded
Long-Term Investors

Monthly growth of wealth ($1), October 1989 – December 2019

One reason for holding bonds is return; the other is they act as a good buffer when share markets fall. The chart shows bond returns in light blue, with only one year, 1994, when both bonds and shares experienced a negative return at the same time.

Bonds as a Buffer

January 1990–December 2019

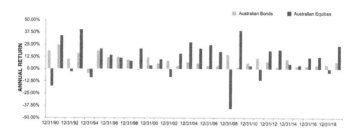

- Shares and bonds perform differently.
- Bonds can act as a kind of cushion or buffer, reducing the ups and downs and giving a smoother ride.

Everyone should have some cash, but a retiree is more likely to need cash and assets in short-term investments to protect their wealth, provide liquidity and ensure their portfolio is protected in a downturn.

Bonds can also be risky, and investors should be aware of risky products promising safe returns.

The days of living solely on interest from a bond have long gone. Lower interest rates have clients asking "Where can I get yield?" The temptation to stretch for high yield could lead an otherwise cautious investor to a bond portfolio that, unintentionally, is as risky as an equity portfolio.

Bond investing fundamentally involves two forms of risk:

1. Credit risk is the risk that a bond issuer will not fully pay the interest on the principal of the bond due to financial distress or bankruptcy.
2. Interest rate risk is the risk that an increase in interest rates will reduce the current market value of

existing bonds. If you buy a bond and then interest rates rise, other investors will demand a discount to buy that bond because it now has a below-market interest rate.

Now that you know why bonds can incur losses, I'll put those losses into a historical perspective. Since 1928, there has only been one year where 10-year government bonds and stocks each lost more than 5 per cent in the same year. In fact, since 1928, 10-year government bonds have lost 5 per cent or more in only five calendar years.

The core bond holding for most investors should be a diversified bond market approach modified to take into account the level of equities an investor holds in the portfolio.

For an investor with a smaller allocation to equities and larger allocation to bonds, the lower return of bonds puts the portfolio at risk of being outpaced by inflation. For an investor with a higher equity allocation and smaller allocation to bonds, the primary role of bonds is to provide diversification when the equity portion of the portfolio sustains a loss. In these portfolios, investors should consider buying longer-term, high credit quality bonds, because historically they have risen and fallen at different times to equities.

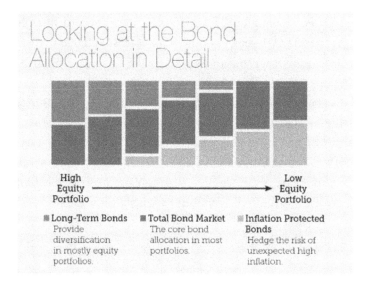

Looking at the Bond Allocation in Detail

High Equity Portfolio → Low Equity Portfolio

- **Long-Term Bonds** Provide diversification in mostly equity portfolios.
- **Total Bond Market** The core bond allocation in most portfolios.
- **Inflation Protected Bonds** Hedge the risk of unexpected high inflation.

A buckets approach to asset allocation

As a general rule, as you get older you want more of your assets in bonds and cash, but this is a general rule only. Some clients have all assets in shares, some all in property, some all in cash for various reasons.

What is important is deciding what level of cash you require, how much you need to draw from your portfolio as income, and how long you can withstand market falls. When share markets fall you have to make sure you don't panic and sell. In fact, that's when you should buy more. The only way to make sure you don't panic is to:

- Have a structure and philosophy
- Diversify
- Make sure you always have enough cash reserves for at least a year — and for retirees it is a good idea to hold five times that amount in cash and bonds.

For example, if I am retired and need to live off $60,000 a year, I should have at least $60,000 in cash or short-term bonds and up to $300,000 in bonds.

Principle 6. Maintaining discipline via rebalancing

Being a successful athlete, performer, businessperson, writer or anything else takes discipline. You have to keep blinkers on and not worry about what the press, crowds or other players are saying. This applies to investing too. There are a million distractions ranging from the press and your friends to what other investors are doing. Gamblers will always boast about their wins and hot tips, but perhaps not disclose their overall performance. We all know that the house has a better chance of winning.

As an investor, you need a lot of discipline.

After a few strong years of returns, will you have the discipline to reduce shares and buy more bonds? Will you read a newspaper article and change strategy? Will you take a tip from a mate or neighbour?

An evidence-based approach to investing takes a lot of self-control. It's not what the investment industry wants: they want you to buy their products and give them your money. The media just want to sell advertising, so why would they cover evidence-based investing? It's not sexy and it certainly does not sell papers. Can you imagine an editor saying to a journalist every day "Write another piece about asset allocation, diversifying and not investing using your emotions"?

"Investing should be more like watching paint dry or watching grass grow. If you want excitement, take $800 and go to Las Vegas." Paul Samuelson - Nobel Prize-winning American economist

There are a lot of forces at play that try to ensure you lose track, and we are some of the worst culprits. Our natural behavioural biases are not wired to be good investors, and we simply can't resist the urge to sell when markets fall and buy when they are high. I talk about this more in chapter 6.

A disciplined rebalancing strategy is an important part of a diversified investment programme. In a given period, asset classes deliver a different performance. As some assets appreciate and others lose value, your portfolio's allocation changes, which affects its risk and return qualities, a condition known as asset class drift or style drift.

The purpose of rebalancing is to move a portfolio back to its original target allocation by following the first rule of investing: buy low and sell high. By selling assets that have risen in value and buying assets that have dropped in value, rebalancing takes the portfolio back to its original allocation. We set percentage bands and rebalance a portfolio when asset levels exceed those predefined limits.

The discipline of rebalancing can reduce portfolio volatility. Remember that you chose your original asset allocation to reflect your personal risk and return preferences for the long term.

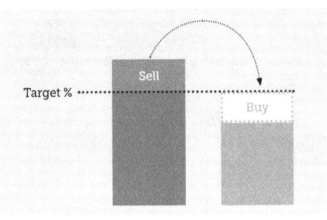

CHAPTER 5 SUMMARY

Here are the central principles of evidence-based investing:

1. The investor or client always comes first
2. A belief in capital markets
3. Risk and reward are related
4. Diversification reduces investment risk
5. Asset allocation is important as it goes a long way to determining performance
6. Maintaining discipline via rebalancing.

6

Understanding Why our Minds are Wired To Make Bad Investment Decisions

"The market is full of people who think they can beat the market, and full of people who believe them. This is one of the greatest mysteries of finance. Why do people believe they can do the impossible? Why do other people believe them?" Daniel Kahneman - Asset Magazine Nov/Dec 1998

As humans, we are wired to make the wrong investment decisions. We all know to buy low and sell high, but when markets fall why are there so many sellers? What is driving this?

The media? Yes, the media has a huge role in fuelling people's fear. But they are just doing their job.

The bigger problem is us — you and me. As investors we just can't help worrying and wanting to do the wrong thing at the wrong time. You know it's illogical, but your mind is telling you to run – a big bear is coming for you and you have to get out!

Despite having all the facts and education, your

emotions can take over and make you do exactly the wrong thing at the wrong time.

Your broker, adviser, friend or whoever helps to guide your investments may be making this worse by fuelling your anxiety and need to sell or buy at the wrong time.

There is a great quote from Eugene Fama, who states that you should not look at your stocks - ever! Why? Well he says if you are worried about a market fall you should never have been there.

This is true - investments work, investors don't.

So how do you avoid making the wrong decisions? The chart below shows the emotional curve of investing. Markets are fuelled by greed and fear and investors buying at the wrong times.

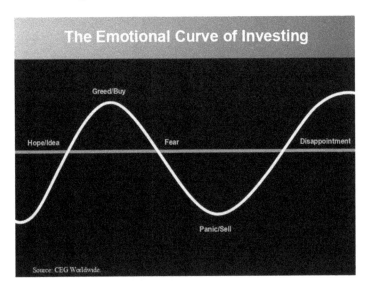

An understanding of the world of behavioural finance may help.

"To invest successfully does not require a stratospheric IQ, unusual business insights, or inside information", Buffett says in the foreword to a revised edition of Benjamin Graham's *The Intelligent Investor*. "What's needed is a sound intellectual framework for making decisions and the ability to keep emotions from corroding the framework."[14]

In 2002 Daniel Kahneman won the Nobel Prize in Economic Sciences for his work in behavioural finance, which is basically understanding how we are wired. His book *Thinking Fast and Slow* was published in 2011 and became a bestseller.

Behavioural finance is a relatively new field that seeks to combine behavioural and cognitive psychological theory with conventional economics and finance to provide explanations for why people make irrational financial decisions.

The problem most investors face, and you're probably one, is that you are wired to act exactly the opposite way when it comes to financial markets.

And the media knows this and plays on it.

Do you recognise this guy in the picture below? Almost every time the market falls there are headlines like "Billions lost today as markets crash", and in many cases I see an image of this guy. I don't know who he is, and I'm not sure if he knows he is in so many newspapers, but I'd like to meet him one day and ask. The point is these headlines and images instil fear and panic. And your instincts make you

---

14 The Intelligent Investor, Benjamin Graham

want to sell. Trader 588 looks worried and he has lost his hair — again!

Source: *The Australian*

With other purchases, for example when you buy a fridge, you look at all the brands and features and buy the fridge that suits your needs. If there are two identical refrigerators and one is $20 cheaper than the other, most people will buy the cheaper fridge.

However when it comes to shares, when there are large discounts (i.e. the market has recently fallen) most people don't want to buy because they're not sure how much lower the price will go or when, or even if the companies they're interested in will survive. You prefer to buy when stock prices are high as you deem it to be safer, more secure. If other investors think the stock is worth X it must be. This is counter-intuitive. What is fuelling this decision is fear.

History has shown that investors don't always act rationally, and this costs investors billions in returns and affects their future.

The problem with investment markets is not the investments, but the investors.

Behavioural finance attempts to understand and explain actual investor behaviour versus theories of investor behaviour.

Emotion and deeply ingrained biases influence our decisions, causing us to behave in unpredictable or irrational ways. In fact, this may be considered predictably irrational.

Cognitive psychologists Daniel Kahneman and Amos Tversky are considered the fathers of behavioural economics/finance.[15] Investors are influenced by two primary behavioural biases: cognitive errors and emotional biases. It's worth exploring these as you'll get a better appreciation of why you are one of millions of Australians handing over your investment management to the 'experts' when, in fact, they're not.

Cognitive Errors

Cognitive errors deal with how people think and result from memory and information-processing errors and are, therefore, the result of faulty reasoning.

There are two sets of cognitive errors: belief perseverance biases and information-processing biases.

---

15 In 2002, Kahneman received the Nobel Memorial Prize in Economic Sciences for his contributions to the study of rationality in economics.

Belief perseverance biases are where people have a hard time modifying their beliefs, even when faced with information to the contrary. They include cognitive dissonance, conservatism, confirmation, representativeness, illusion of control and hindsight.

Information-processing biases are where people make errors in their thinking when processing information related to a financial decision. They include anchoring and adjustment, mental accounting, framing, availability, self-attribution, outcome and recency.

Emotional Biases

Emotional biases are the result of reasoning influenced by feelings.

It is a very human reaction to feel mentally uncomfortable when new facts contradict information you previously held to be true – a psychological phenomenon known as cognitive dissonance.

For example, 2,000 years after the Greek philosopher Pythagoras suggested the world was round, Columbus was still trying to refute the common belief that it was flat by attempting to circumnavigate the globe.

Emotional biases are based on feelings rather than facts. Emotions often overpower our thinking during times of stress. All of us will have made irrational decisions at some time. Emotional biases include loss aversion, overconfidence, self-control, status quo, endowment, regret aversion and affinity.

Behavioural Finance in Practice

Investors often go to great lengths to rationalise decisions on prior investments, especially failed investments. They will in effect tell their mind that it is ok. This can lead to irrational behaviour and holding on to a poor investment.

In both cases, the effects of cognitive dissonance are preventing investors from acting rationally and even preventing them from realising losses for tax purposes and reallocating at the earliest opportunity. For example, many investors will hold a share due to an attachment even though it has dropped considerably in value. They may have worked at the company, or it may have been part of an inheritance.

Furthermore, and perhaps even more importantly, pride may prevent investors from learning from their mistakes, so they often attribute their failures to luck rather than poor decision-making.

You are not a robot and you can't always control your emotions as no one is perfect, but to be a successful investor it is important to know how these factors influence your decisions.

Effective ways to avoid letting emotions take control are:

- Have an investment policy.
- Find ways to keep your investment process disciplined.
- Ensure any change is well thought through and aligns with your policy and philosophy.
- Keep your long-term goal in mind.
- Use the media for entertainment, not to make your investment decisions.

- Be wary of anyone, especially a fund manager or investor newsletter, who says they can forecast the future.

An easy mistake to make, and I've made it

Your friend from university has just started a new business and is offering a once in a lifetime opportunity to invest. It sounds exciting and he only has a few shares available.

So, do you:

- Invest all your money — let's go all in, we are going to be rich.
- Invest a large amount of money — after all this guy is smart. It's worth backing him.
- Invest a very small amount. It's a token and it won't make you rich, but it's a bit of fun.
- Just simply wish him well and say thank you. Explain politely that this type of seed or venture capital speculation doesn't fit into your family investment strategy; you have a responsibility to yourself and your family to invest for the long term and stay disciplined. Your friend will respect this decision and just move through his sales pipeline to the next mate, I promise you, and he will not hold this against you. If he does he is not a friend.

The best answer is always no 4, or maybe on a very few occasions 3 (and I'm talking about a very small percentage of your investment).

CHAPTER 6 SUMMARY

» The fear and greed portrayed in the media influences us and can lead to poor investment decisions.

» Understanding and being aware of our emotions can help avoid these mistakes.

» By simply managing the aspects we can control, and letting markets work, investors will be generally better off. Investors, rather than investment markets, tend to be the biggest detriment on investment performance. Don't let your emotions get in the way of capital market returns that are there for the taking.

» Avoid promises of above normal returns , these advertisements are playing on your emotions.

» Stick to a sound and disciplined investment structure, and avoid the mistakes most investors make who try to guess what will happen in the future, change course frequently, and pay a premium for this emotional roller-coaster.

7

Some data and facts about stock picking and market timing

"By the time a paper is published, you're probably looking at the 200th draft." Eugene F. Fama

Many investors rely on stock picking, market timing and forecasting, however there are decades of research and data showing that this is an unreliable method to seek outperformance.

In the past, many fund investment managers tried to pick stocks and time the market to add value. These investment managers are broadly categorised as active managers, which means that typically they:

- Attempt to outperform the market with stock selection or market timing
- Trade frequently
- Have relatively high costs (in Australian funds the average costs are around 1 per cent)
- Often have a 'star' manager whose ability to outperform they promote.

Their value proposition was and still is:

"Give your money to me and we will make you more money than anyone else"

or

"We are the best fund managers so give us your money."

Their marketing has been based on performance and a unique skill or guru ability, often called 'Alpha'. They forecast the future and tell you that you should invest with them because they know exactly what is going to happen in markets.

"The number of managers that can successfully pick stocks is fewer than you'd expect by chance. So, why even play that game? You don't need to." David Booth, Founder Dimensional

I'm not saying that this is impossible or that these managers are evil or corrupt. All I am pointing out is that there is little evidence to suggest that this is the best way to manage most people's money for the long term, particularly since the research provided by Standard and Poor's is publicly available.[16]

If you put 50 fund managers in a room, explain that mathematically not all of them can outperform, and ask "How many of you will outperform this year?" Guess what? They will all put up their hands. They have to as that is their value proposition. But of course, mathematically, they can't all outperform.

There is a buyer and seller to each trade. Over time,

---

16 https://au.spindices.com/spiva/#/

in a large market with billions of trades every year, it's a zero-sum game. If every manager is investing in the same market, that means if there is one apple, then you can only have one apple less your costs. The fund with higher costs will perform worse than the manager with lower costs most of the time. There is less than a 1 per cent chance of selecting the high-cost manager that wins. Any outperformance is nullified by efficient markets and costs. In reality, many funds don't actually survive, as when they underperform they are merged or closed.

If you are lucky enough to find a manager who does outperform, then you have to hope they can maintain this and survive .

Standard & Poor's have documented research on the survivorship of funds showing that not only is it hard to outperform, but, if you do, your chances of staying at the top are very slight, which reduces your possibility of success considerably.

The data on active trading professional investment managers is well documented and compelling.

Now you may be reading this as a fund manager or may have invested in a fund that has performed well. Excellent, as this is exactly what should happen: some funds should and will outperform.

The question to the fund manager is: how do I know you will continue to outperform? Why should I let clients pay you 1 per cent when I can access funds charging 0.2 per cent for the same exposure and there is no reliable way of confirming what you tell me? That is not a responsible way to invest a client's money — asking them to pay 1 per cent for a hopeful outcome at best.

And the answer to the investor willing to pay managers high fees for the privilege, well, here is the data showing that it's just not a risk worth taking,

Below we show the data across global markets showing that active managers struggle to beat their benchmarks. It is not saying they can't beat the benchmark; the evidence across many markets and segments of markets just shows how hard it is. Of course each year some managers outperform, but not the same ones year in, year out. When we look at this data, we can only conclude that active managers have a role to play, but are they the best place for your money?

All data in the images below are for the 5-year period to 31 December 2019

Australia:
80.79 per cent of active managers underperformed over the 5-year period.

Image source https://au.spindices.com/spiva/#/

United States:
80.6 percent of active managers underperformed.

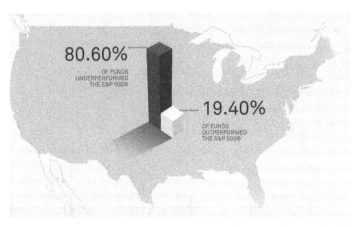

Image source https://au.spindices.com/spiva/#/

Europe:
77.54 per cent of managers underperformed.

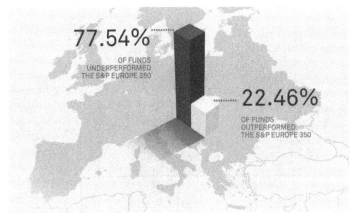

Image source https://au.spindices.com/spiva/#/

Canada:
88%per cent of active managers underperformed.

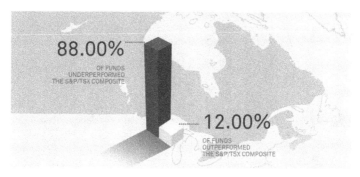

Image source https://au.spindices.com/spiva/#/

What about market timing - is that a good strategy?

The data below shows how much return you can lose if you miss a few of the better trading days.

Between 2001 and 2018, if you missed 10 of the best days on the market your return would have been 5.82% compared to a market return of 8.45%. The charts also illustrate that if you missed the best 25 days you return would have been 2.82% when the bank bill index returned 4.14%. This means you could basically leave your money in cash and have a better return.

Market timing is very risky, hard to do, and you need to consider carefully if it is worth the risk.

It is tempting to try and time markets, but there is just not enough evidence to suggest that it is a reliable strategy.

The biggest winners out of market timing are the funds that charge huge fees promising high returns using this strategy.

Performance of the ASX/S&P 300 Index, 2001–2019

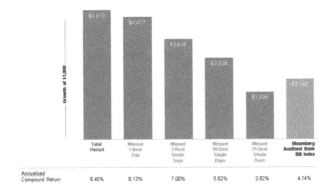

	Total Period	Missed 1 Best Day	Missed 5 Best Single Days	Missed 10 Best Single Days	Missed 25 Best Single Days	Bloomberg AusBond Bank Bill Index
Annualised Compound Return	8.45%	8.13%	7.00%	5.82%	2.82%	4.14%

Image from Dimensional Fund Advisors

There is not much evidence to suggest that managing your own money by stock picking or trying to select an active manager is the most successful way to invest. Then why do so many people try to invest using this methodology?

There are thousands of very smart, sophisticated fund managers struggling to beat the industry benchmarks year in year out using a stock-picking approach. Some do, some don't, but the problem is there is no way to identify in advance the very few who do, and then there is no way to ensure that the manager continues to outperform. A few will outperform every year, but not necessarily the same ones as the next year. You need to be lucky, and what we want to achieve is successful investment outcomes that remove luck.

Compelling evidence shows this style of investing or stock picking has not rewarded most investors in the long run.

Trying to time which market to be in at any time to improve returns, otherwise called market timing, is difficult, expensive and nerve-racking.

Here is a chart showing just how hard this is. The chart shows the best performing asset classes each year, and ranks them to the worst performing.

Periodic Table of Assets—AUD

January 2003–December 2019

Can you see a pattern? Is it easy to tell which asset class will be the winner next year?

Now let's look at this chart, which breaks the data into even more detail and country regions.

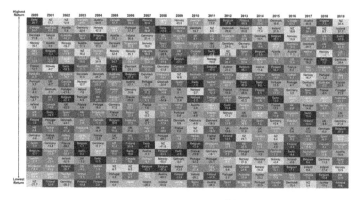

Images sourced from Dimensional Fund Advisors

Any easier now to know which sector or region will be the best in the future?

There is, of course, no pattern. Markets are unpredictable and there is no clear-cut way to predict which market segment will beat another, year in, year out. The table below shows the data again, and just how random the returns are from year to year.

Equity Returns of Developed Markets—AUD
Annual Return (%)

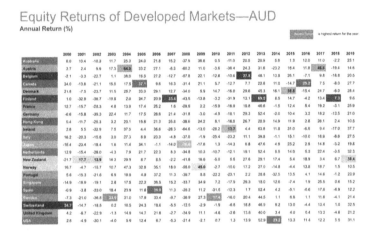

There have also been studies showing that, if you do try and market time, what can happen if you miss a few good days.

This chart shows the impact on performance if you miss the top 10 per cent of performers each year.

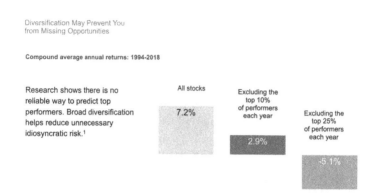

Diversification May Prevent You
from Missing Opportunities

Compound average annual returns: 1994-2018

Research shows there is no
reliable way to predict top
performers. Broad diversification
helps reduce unnecessary
idiosyncratic risk.[1]

All stocks

7.2%

Excluding the
top 10%
of performers
each year

2.9%

Excluding the
top 25%
of performers
each year

-5.1%

So if you happen to miss just a few days or a few stocks, your long term return is substantially reduced.

Market timing and stock picking are just not worth the risk for long-term investors, and your chances of success using stock picking from home or through a broker or a manager are very slim.

Why is it so hard for an active manager to outperform?

The reason stock picking and market timing don't work is not because these managers aren't smart enough. In fact, some are so smart they make the problem worse for themselves.

The reason is that markets are very efficient, but if they were not efficient they would have no credibility and no one would trust them.

So if a market is very efficient, then the prices are fair, and if the prices are fair and we trust the market mechanism, then we will buy, right?

Now the counter-argument is that markets are not perfectly efficient so you can use that inefficiency to gain an advantage and outperform by stock picking. Yes, there are pockets of inefficiency, but still the data shows very few professional managers who have managed to exploit them — the primary reason being that the costs of exploiting this advantage are too high, and it is also very hard to do over a long period.

In fact if all stock pickers could all add value over time, this would mean that the market was actually not fair and could have no credibility. A market without credibility would not be trusted or traded, and then we would have no market.

So the market needs to be relatively fair to continue to exist.

Markets generally work. As investors we are better off assuming that they work well, because to be a successful investor we need to embrace market pricing.

The market is an effective information-processing machine. Each day, the world equity markets process billions of dollars in trades between buyers and sellers—and the real-time information they bring helps set prices.

In Australian dollars. Source: Dimensional, using data from Bloomberg LP. Includes primary and secondary exchange trading volume globally for equities. ETFs and funds are excluded. Daily averages were computed by calculating the trading volume of each stock daily on the closing price multiplied by shares traded that day. All such trading volume is summed up and divided by 252 as an approximate number of actual trading days.

This pricing power of markets works against managed funds that try to outperform by stock picking or market timing. Because they are trying to outguess the market, they lose most of the time, and then they don't survive the corporate axe. Between 1999 and 2018 only 42 per cent of US equity managers and only 41 per cent of fixed income or bond funds survived.

You simply should not be playing this game if you want to have a successful portfolio over time.

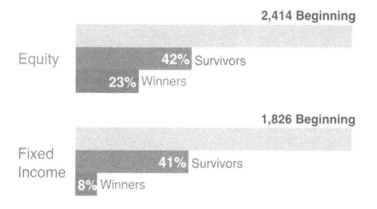

The reality and practicality are if you are managing money, and trying to pick stocks based on information you hope that no one else has or has identified, then you may get one or two great picks every few months or years. But is that sustainable and will it add much value after costs?

There are so many trades each day, so much information that the hope that an active manager can add value by using this information to their advantage is irrational.

This concept can be very hard for investors to accept since they are seeking an opportunity or advantage over every other investor. Surely they are smarter than the market? Surely it's obvious that this stock is going to be a great pick? You can try this approach, but the data from the past is not too encouraging. Rest assured this style of investing will always exist, because someone will always be overconfident, or get a bit lucky and confuse luck with skill.

"Forecasts may tell you a great deal about the forecaster; they tell you nothing about the future." Warren Buffet

As investors, we all want fair and efficient markets. This is capitalism; the alternative doesn't work.

There is also the temptation to chase the past performers. If we look at the data we also see that some funds did outperform over the past five years. So why not just choose them?

Well, if only it were that simple. The data show the funds that outperform do not stay on top of the rankings. Unfortunately, past performance provides little insight into future performance. Of the 23 per cent that did outperform, five years later only 21 per cent had stayed on top, so this implies about a 5 per cent chance of a fund staying on top — if it survives. And since a lot of funds don't survive due to corporate buyouts, mergers, retirement, etc., the chance of selecting the best manager is even smaller.

Is the risk worth taking?

Percentage of Top-Ranked US Funds That Stayed on Top

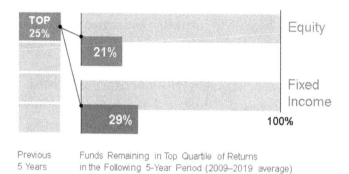

Previous 5 Years — Funds Remaining in Top Quartile of Returns in the Following 5-Year Period (2009–2019 average)

So we have a few principles learned from the past to guide us to become better investors:

- Market prices are a very good reflection of what an investment is worth. Billions of trades a day provide this mechanism.
- Trying to pick stocks is an inefficient way to manage money, with little chance of success over the long term.
- Timing the market is difficult and expensive. The risk of missing a few days that make a big difference zeros out as a potential benefit.

You are investing in a capitalist system, so unless that fails you invest to get a better return on your money over time.

If from reading this book so far you agree with the principles that:

- You are a long-term investor.
- You believe in markets, and agree that market pricing is very efficient, though I am not saying perfect!
- You understand that risk and return are related.
- You realise that the data shows that it is very difficult to outperform by picking stocks or selecting an active fund manager.

Then investing has become easier for you because you realise there is a different, better way to invest that does not rely on forecasting, stick picking or superstar fund managers.

Remember, anyone claiming they know exactly what the future looks like in the investment game is simply trying to take your money and put it in their pocket.

"Wall Street's favourite scam is pretending luck is skill."
Ron Ross[17]

There are some more reasons why it's really hard to add value by picking stocks or markets:

- No one knows the future.
- To try and bet on the future adds to your costs.
- These costs come in the form of higher transaction costs, analysis, and marketing.

17 The Unbeatable Market: Taking the Indexing Path to Financial Peace of Mind - Ron Ross

- Using this approach means fewer holdings, so if you get it wrong... you are in trouble.
- Being less diversified adds huge risk.

CHAPTER 7 SUMMARY

» Picking stocks and market timing are a highly unreliable way to achieve investment success. That relies on forecasting and taking guesses.

» Even if you do get lucky picking a stock or a fund manager, there is not a great chance of this success being repeated.

» However, trying to guess what will happen is tempting and will always be as a way to invest as investors and fund managers will always want to believe they can outperform. It's a highly lucrative business, so there is plenty of financial incentive to 'have a crack' and see how you go. As investors, you simply need to be aware of this and make informed decisions.

8

A Quick Story About Investing in a Startup. And Hedge Funds

"Are you willing to sell someone a shoe that doesn't fit? Or are you willing to lose a sale because you don't have the right size?" David Booth

A recent client understood the need for a sensible investment approach, but had a mate who had invested in a small mining company and the shares were worth a fortune.

How does this fit into a portfolio?

My simple and honest answer was:

- You worked hard to build up your assets and investments. For the rest of your life, you need these assets to work for you. One of your prime goals is to preserve your wealth
- Your key objective is to generate a reliable income for the rest of your life for yourself and your family.
- Nowhere in our conversation have you mentioned, not once, that you want to use your hard-earned money to line the pockets of your mates (other than shout the odd beer at the golf club).

- You said above all you want to look after your family and, hopefully, leave a legacy for them.

So what has changed, and why are you changing your goals?

You can achieve your investment goals simplistically using two approaches:

- By gambling/guesswork — buying a few hot tips like the mining company
- By investing sensibly, capturing market returns and using science to try and do a bit better than the market while reducing risk, as well as removing all worry and guesswork from the investment process.

Market returns are there for the taking, but most people miss out.

Of course many Australians like a punt, so by all means have a punt – but that is what the casino is for or Sportsbet. Don't bet your life savings.

In fact, the term blue chip comes from the game of poker where blue chips have the highest value…

A quick word about – hedge funds

A hedge fund is a managed fund that can do anything really! It's a broad term used for funds that take strategies to time markets, trade currencies or pick stocks — or all of them.

The problem is that hedge funds typically charge 2 per cent plus performance fees of 20 per cent. That's called the 2 and 20 trade. They are also generally illiquid, which means it's hard to get your money out if you want to.

The data shows performance that is volatile with some huge outperformers and huge underperformers, however interestingly as a whole the average returns are around the longer term bond market return, and bonds are generally speaking a much safer investment compared to hedge funds. However hedge funds are generally quite risky.

Of course some funds have performed very well, but a lot have failed completely and lost all the investors' money. One of the most famous hedge funds was run by Bernie Madoff. Unfortunately it ended up being the largest Ponzi scheme ever and Bernie was sentenced to jail for 150 years. A Ponzi scheme is a fraudulent investing scam promising high rates of return with little risk to investors. The Ponzi scheme generates returns for early investors by acquiring new investors and effectively using new funds to pay out to earlier investors.

The chance of picking a hedge fund that has a very high rate of return is as slim as finding an active manager.

The conclusion: most investors don't need hedge funds to reach their goals.

If used at all they should be a very small part of a portfolio.

Before you invest in a hedge fund, decide who you think is benefiting the most. You or the hedge fund manager?

CHAPTER 8 SUMMARY

» Once you adopt evidence-based investing, it will be hard to say no to a mate or an investment that sounds amazing. But that is ok.

» Most of the time, if it sounds too good to be true, it probably is.

» Keep your and your family's investment goals in mind before making any one-off investments.

9

Giving you the academic advantage

"It's just fun to do the research, learn new stuff, and potentially have an impact on the way people are thinking about the world." Kenneth R. French

When we look at the various ways to invest, we can break them down into two distinct groups or philosophies. One relies on forecasting and the other relies on market prices. The academic research has been a gift to us all, and it is really up to us as investors whether we choose to accept it.

A very brief history of indexing
Investing in the broader market has been a concept for over 50 years. When Jack Bogle founded Vanguard in the 1970s he was mocked by his peers. Why would you invest in the market when you could 'outperform' by picking stocks?

Vanguard today has approximately US$6trillion assets, making it the largest asset manager in the world.

Bogle was a pioneer, and not only has Vanguard succeeded but there are many other index-style managers globally.

Despite the evidence, investors, perhaps you, still hang on to poor investment solutions and chase other ideas. It doesn't make sense.

Scientists are still trying to work this out!

Forecasting

The conventional or most commonly used method until recently relies on forecasting or using a star fund manager who is promoted as having an amazing stock picking ability, or following the approach of another famous stock picker.

This style of investment has the following characteristics:

- Concentrated positions, i.e. relatively few holdings or a focus on a certain industry or geographical area
- Higher costs
- High turnover
- Poor tax management
- Plenty of advertising.

It's a success story, but for end investors in the flagship fund returns have been worse than simply investing in the broader market. Yes, there were times in the early days when Platinum performed, but was this skill or luck?

If you had invested in the Vanguard index fund that charges .05 per cent over the same period of time, you would have had a better outcome as Platinum charges 1.35 per cent.

There is a role for Platinum, but should it be in almost every portfolio in the country? They take bets, sometimes big bets, and charge a high premium. That is their role, however at most Platinum should be a small allocation of a retiree's portfolio, and not the only international exposure.

Like some fund managers, the Platinum team are smart managers and very wealthy, so there is an appeal to getting on board and benefiting from their 'smarts'. But, if you look at it logically and with reference to academic research, what they achieved is exactly what the academics would predict. As I have already explained in this book, the data show us that most active fund managers don't perform, but those that do — and mathematically some have to — get excited and then market this out-performance heavily. Eventually their luck runs out as they simply can't outperform every year. Sometimes it's luck, sometimes their ego and sometimes they make bets they should not be making. Regardless, the statistics show that very few fund managers outperform.

You may get lucky and pick a star manager like Platinum, but when they underperform you are stuck in a very expensive fund.

It's not just Platinum; this is a global predicament. Standard & Poor's measures the performance of fund managers, and year after year the numbers are similar. Most managers don't beat their benchmark.

Now you could say, well I'll pick the winners, but unfortunately not only is this difficult — how do you know in advance — but the evidence shows that the underperforming manager is not likely to go back to outperforming.

So why bother? Well, until now you did not have much choice. No one told you about the alternative.

The academic or evidence-based approach

The different way to invest is using science and research. This method relies on some common principles:

- A belief in markets
- Diversification
- Risk and return are related
- Very little or no reliance on forecasts
- Reasonable costs
- Fund survival is important
- Tax management is important.
- Giving investors more peace of mind and less to worry about. Investors don't need to know what is happening in markets to have a successful investment experience.

You may find it hard to believe that academics started to develop this way of investing as far back as the 1930s, but it wasn't until 1976 that a broad-based market index fund was available to the public. The take-up was quite slow as the existing investment community continued to promote their performance and ability to 'outperform' heavily. As data improved and regulation also forced better disclosure, index style funds took off and are now the largest managers in the world.

If you want to be a long-term investor, using an investing strategy gives you a greater chance of success — and also less anxiety. It leads to a better understanding of where returns come from, better expectations, and better asset allocation decisions.

"Dimensional's investment philosophy is about more than returns—it's about a great client experience that can really help people relax." David Booth

The market will provide a return whether you like it or not. The foundation for long-term success for a portfolio is not trying to pick a guru, but to ensure you:

- Have an asset allocation that suits you
- Have a plan
- Understand markets
- Capture market returns as efficiently as you can
- Enhance returns via structure and tilting to academically proven dimensions of the market in a very diversified manner.

"My regular recommendation has been a low-cost S&P 500 index fund," Buffett wrote in his 2016 Berkshire Hathaway annual shareholder letter.[18]

---

18 Business insider.com Dec 2019

The Academic Journey:

From Bogle, Fama and French to the latest - why these smart minds have provided a gift for you

The chart below shows a timeline of sustainable academic development into finance. As investors we are fortunate that these economists have reviewed data and performance over the decades and worked out a better way to invest.

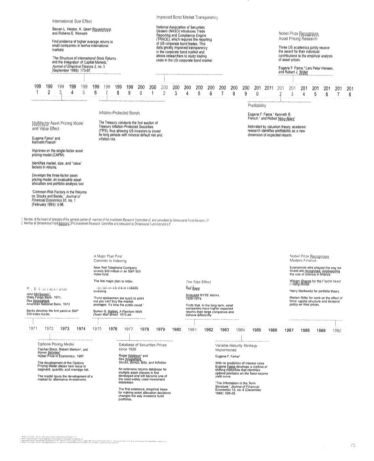

Decades of evidence show that thousands of highly intelligent fund managers all over the world have struggled to beat the benchmark or index. Why?

Over the past half-century economists have worked out a better way. It all started in the late 1950s in Chicago, but it was not until the 1960s that research papers were published.

Of course data back then was limited and computers were the size of a house, so it was not easy to prove a point and it took time!

On 31 August 1976, Vanguard, which now manages over US$6 trillion dollars[19], launched the world's first index fund.

Vanguard founder Jack Bogle was not the only one espousing this idea, but was the first to market it.

Economists were realising that just buying and holding the broad stock market would provide better results than trying to beat it by picking stocks.

Of course this met with derision from Wall Street, which made money from trading in stocks, or more precisely the fees they charged for trading in stocks.

In 1951, for his undergraduate thesis at Princeton University, John C. Bogle conducted a study which found that most mutual funds did not earn any more money than if they invested in broad stock market indices

Even if the stocks in the funds beat the benchmark index, management fees reduced the returns to investors below the returns of the benchmark.

In 1966 Eugene Fama's Efficient Market hypothesis was

19 Assets under management data sourced from vanguard.com

a huge moment in the development of finance as we know it today. Fama went on to win a Nobel Prize in 2013. He basically discovered that security prices reflect all available information.

In 1973 Robert Merton, who was awarded the Nobel Prize in Economic Sciences in 1997, explained to the world how multiple sources of risk could occur.

Merton's research focuses on finance theory, including lifecycle finance, optimal intertemporal portfolio selection, capital asset pricing, pricing of options, risky corporate debt, loan guarantees and other complex derivative securities. His own hedge fund, Long Term Capital Management (LTCM), collapsed spectacularly, but he added how risks are related to academic findings and, in my view, also showed us all that even the very smartest professionals should not try to second guess the market.

To reiterate this point, Vanguard manages over $6 trillion dollars today, while LTCM went bust.

In 1981 David Booth, who founded Dimensional Fund Advisors, pioneered small-cap investing in a diversified manner. It actually took many years for the fund to show value, and Dimensional struggled to sell the idea, but they persevered and are today the pioneers of low-cost, evidence-based investing, managing in excess of A$800 billion.

In 1983 Eugene Fama's research showed that forward interest rates provide information on elected term premiums in fixed interest.

In 1992 Fama and Ken French discovered the 'value breakthrough', and developed a three-factor model to prove assets, identifying market size and price/value as the principal drivers of equity returns.

In 2012 Fama, with French and Robert Novy Marx, added profitability as a dimension to expected returns.

There are now decades of research and data to help you to avoid the mistakes of the past.

This research allows investors to sift through all the financial papers and journals to uncover the truth and learn a better way to invest.

The priority of all investors is to capture market returns, and then an extra dimension of returns in a structured way that keeps costs reasonable.

Today economists around the world watch markets constantly, and new findings emerge. There are big ideas out there, and highly intelligent people are working on all possible scenarios, opportunities and threats, even outliers such as coronavirus.

If you have lost trust in our banks and other financial companies, or you want more control over your future, you can use knowledge and insights from the worlds of finance and academia.

The challenge for the industry is to let the past go and move forward with a much simpler model, but that would be the end of fees so it's unlikely to happen. However, you don't need to wait. You can manage your financial future like this now.

Dimensional Fund Advisors, based in Texas with 13 offices worldwide and A$739 billion under management, is an excellent example of a fund manager that has developed a business using the best ideas from finance and smart implementation with the objective of rewarding investors with better than index returns at very reasonable costs. It's a great story. As well as delivering successful outcomes, they have never closed a fund and never paid a commission. They have a strong presence in the Asia Pacific with offices in Sydney and Melbourne for Australian investors.

The chart below compares conventional or active managers to index managers and to an alternative approach like Dimensional's.

Conventional Management
- Attempts to identify mispricing in securities
- Relies on forecasting to select "undervalued" securities or time markets
- Generates higher expenses, trading costs, and risks

Index Management
- Allows commercial index to determine strategy
- Attempts to match index performance, restricting which securities to hold and when to trade
- Prioritizes low tracking error over higher expected returns

An Alternate Approach
- Gains insights about markets and returns from academic research
- Structures portfolios along the dimensions of expected returns
- Adds value by integrating research, portfolio structure, and implementation

CHAPTER 9 SUMMARY

» Decades of data and academic research can point us in the right direction.

» Economists are unbiased and would be equally happy to prove that stock picking is a great way to invest.

» We can use this information or ignore it.

10

How this knowledge can help you become a better investor

"This investment approach is easy to communicate, is verifiable, and is eminently defensible." Rex Sinquefield

This knowledge shows many people how to become a better investor.

The industry in Australia has not served you well. There have been too many conflicts. Costs have been too high. Investors have had limited access to the truth and many investors know little about finance. No wonder this has led to poor outcomes.

We can start by improving the financial literacy of all Australians. This is a big goal, and I want to make the information available. At the very least, more Australians should simply have their superannuation invested in low-cost, asset-based funds.

When I came across this academic approach and met with Dimensional Fund Advisors in 2002, I was excited and relieved. I was relieved because I had been thinking of leaving the industry, and now there was a reason to stay. I was so disappointed that the industry was full of advisers and planners just selling products that I had decided it was not for me. The culture and the people did not align with my values.

Meeting Dimensional showed me that at least one major institution was in the business of working out the right solution for clients.

I was excited and I wanted to go out there and tell my clients before anyone else did! I thought every adviser would meet Dimensional and work this out pretty quickly.

It is now 2020 and no new client I meet has ever heard of Dimensional, even though most of them have worked with other planners or invested through a major institution or super fund.

This amazes me, but it's my mission to share this knowledge.

I wanted the best outcome for my clients following a long-term investment strategy, and the only way to meet all my requirements of client care and governance as well as ensuring clients received the proper returns was to implement the best possible financial methods at low cost and with no conflict.

The only way I could achieve this was by implementing this evidence-based approach.

Sticking to a long-term investor evidence-based approach has been challenging. It would have been a lot easier to sell commission-based products just like almost everyone else in the industry, and probably more financially rewarding in the short term. But it was not the right thing to do.

The good news is that you no longer need to believe what most of the investment and financial community tell you, because you now know the truth about investments.

Now you know there is a different and better way to invest, you no longer have to pay high investment costs for underperformance.

Investing using science not guesswork can make a huge difference to your wealth and to your life.

Using academic research from the past and present is a different way to invest, and it delivers better outcomes for most people than the conventional methods of stock picking.

The reasons are:

- The old way is more expensive, and your chances of success are slim.
- The evidence based approach gives you a very good chance of success over the long term due to more reasonable costs, less turnover, better discipline and structure.
- There is a far greater chance that your investment funds will survive and be around in 30 years.

Here is some more data showing that this is a global trend and the data and evidence only improve over time:

This is from bloomberg.com. demonstrating the net flows out of active funds and net flows into passive or index funds:

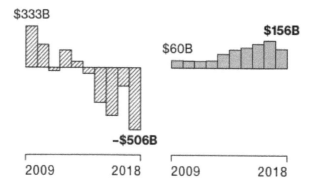

This chart shows the percentage of funds in index/passive funds with the US leading the way:

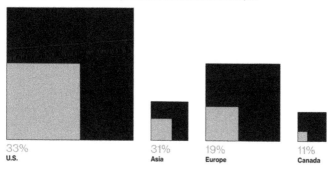

Data and graphs from bloomberg.com and morningstar

CHAPTER 10 SUMMARY

» There is a huge trend in global markets for money moving towards evidence-based investing.

» You may be confident that using science rather than guesswork is well documented and proven to work, and it also puts you, the investor, first.

11

A process for ensuring investment success

"Control what you can control." Dave Butler

To be a successful investor requires a sound process and following principles to keep you on track.

In this chapter we go through a step-by-step guide to develop your strategy, followed by 10 investment principles.

Developing Your Investment Strategy

Step 1. Assess your goals and circumstances.
The investment plan process begins with a discussion of your financial values and goals, and your most important relationships, existing assets, other professional advisors, preferred process, and important interests.

Take some time where you can think with no distractions, and ask yourself — what is important about money to me?

If you have a partner do this together, but answer the question separately.

List the answers here:

1. . . . .

2. . . . .

3. . . . .

4. . . . .

5. . . . .

Step 2. Set long-term investment objectives.
- What are your long-term investment goals?
- Is there anyone else you need to take care of: children, parents, sisters, brothers, aunts?
- What do you want to do when you retire?
- When do you want to retire?
- How much income do you think you will need? Not many people know, so the best starting point is what your after-tax income is now.

Taking into account the long-term nature of successful investing, set objectives for your portfolio that are appropriate for your willingness, ability and need to take risk, and the investment horizon(s) you identify.

Write out these investment goals here:

1 . . . .

2 . . . .

3 . . . .

4 . . . .

5 . . . .

6 . . . .

A tip for goals – ensure you use a SMART framework.

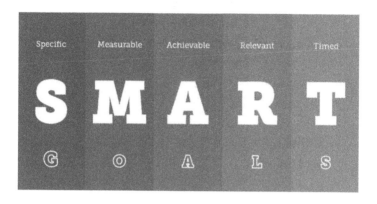

Step 3. Plan your asset allocation

Because it is so important, asset allocation is the first investment decision.

Establish your attitude to risk to determine how much of your portfolio to invest in each of the different investment types or asset classes, including shares, bonds and short-term investments, both domestic and international.

- Step one is to allocate funds to cash.
- Step two is to allocate a percentage to bonds.
- Step Three is to allocate a percentage to growth assets (shares and property).

Write out your asset allocation here in dollars or percentages.

Example Allocation

- Cash required for rainy day
- Cash required for one year's income

- Bonds (up to 5 x annual income if retired)
- Shares - Australian Large
- Shares - Australian Value
- Shares - Australian Small
- Shares - Global Large
- Shares - Global Value
- Shares - Global Small
- Shares - Emerging Markets
- Property
    Direct
    Listed
- Other

For asset allocation examples, or if you need help, we provide contacts and references in our appendix.

Step 4. Select your investment approach
With an asset allocation in place, select the investment vehicles that you will use to implement your portfolio strategy.

Two cardinal investing principles guide these decisions: the importance of diversification and the value of remaining invested.

I recommend you use an evidence-based approach.

There are three broad choices:

Conventional management
- Attempts to identify mispricing in securities
- Relies on forecasting to select 'undervalued' securities or time markets
- Generates higher expenses, trading costs and risks.

Index management
- Allows a commercial index to determine strategy
- Attempts to match index performance, restricting which securities to hold and when to trade
- Prioritizes low tracking error over higher expected returns.

An evidence-based approach:
- Gains insights about markets and returns from academic research
- Structures portfolios along the dimensions of expected returns
- Adds value by integrating research, portfolio structure and implementation.

Step 5. Document and build your portfolio

Building on the first four steps, construct a portfolio suited to your needs, goals, investment horizon and risk attitude. It is important to document this process.

The typical building blocks for the portfolio are institutional asset class managed funds and index managed funds, which are an excellent way to implement a diversified portfolio investment and maximise the probability of achieving your goals. An exchange-traded fund is a managed fund that can be traded on the stock exchange. You should also take into account portfolio costs and the potential tax impact of the restructuring.

12

10 Investment Principles

"Success is not final; failure is not fatal: It is the courage to continue that counts." Winston S. Churchill

10 Investment Principles that will keep you on track

Over the past 20 years, I have met many people who should have been far better off financially than they were. They had high incomes, but because they spent more than they earned they were in an 'income trap'. They never had money to invest so had to keep working, living in the present, rather than thinking about how they were going to live in the future.

And I've had many conversations with clients who earned well over $500,000 a year to show them where their money was going, only for them to say "But I can't spend less."

It's a very common trap that high-level executives fall into. I'm not here to say don't have a great lifestyle, but I do believe in making sure that whether you have a high income, a low income, a business or an inheritance, you know the truth about investing and how to invest wisely.

My main role for my wealthiest client was to keep the piranhas away — I was effectively a gatekeeper and each day all the biggest brokers and dealers in town called me. If this client had not used me as a barrier, she would have lost a lot of money. I was in most cases appalled at how unsophisticated these big brand brokers and dealers were. It was all a charade.

For anyone who wants to invest better and smarter, whether you have lots of money or not much, these principles will help you understand more about how the investment industry works and how to come first. You should come first: it's your money, not theirs.

My investment principles are well documented and researched, and provide a mechanism for you to learn more.

One vital message is: no one really knows what is going to happen. Most forecasts are wrong, simply because no one knows what the future holds. So how many investments are based on forecasts that are likely to be wrong?

The good news is you do not need to have a stratospheric IQ or incredible ability to know what will happen in the future to have a successful investment outcome.

There is a way to do better, although a small percentage of investors will get lucky — but we are not in that game.

I remember sitting on an expert panel early in 2002, and one of the best-known fund managers at the time had this caption on every slide: "expect low returns for the next 10 years". The following few years Australian shares had the following returns:

2003   15.9 per cent

2004   27.6 per cent

2005   21.1 per cent

2006   25 per cent

2007   18 per cent.

With hindsight, many experts predicted the downturn in 2008, but I can assure you that, at the time, not many did.

In 2020 many people expected markets to stall or come down from their heights, but did anyone predict what would happen in March 2020? Unexpected events will happen again, and there is only one way to invest to manage these random events with any chance of success.

The following 10 principles show you how to weather current and future market events, good and bad, with peace of mind thanks to an evidence-based approach to investments. And when other people worry about which stock to be in or what the latest tip is, you can simply relax.

Principle One
Embrace market prices.

You do not need forecasts or predictors for a successful investment experience. The market is a very effective information processing machine

Ignore anyone predicting anything. They could be right. They could also be wrong. There is a good chance they are trying to take your money and put it in their own pocket. A very good chance.

If they are right, they got lucky. It's not a reliable way to invest your life savings.

Principle Two

"Your investment portfolio should be as boring as watching the paint dry." Paul Samuelson

Don't try and outguess the market or overcomplicate your investments.

As part of our consultative client meetings, I ask clients what they want to achieve with their money. In most cases they reply:

- To ensure they can travel
- To have a great lifestyle
- To renovate their house
- To educate their grandkids
- To sail and play golf.

I have never, in almost 20 years, heard:

"I want to watch the market all day for the next 30 years and trade using my online broker account."

Your investments should be boring and safe.

Watching and worrying about investment markets is a fruitless exercise.

Also, just think about this. Suppose you do happen to pick a great active fund manager. What difference will they make to your life? Well, the very few managers who have outperformed only do so by a small margin, so it won't change your life regardless. But, if they mess it up, then the impact is huge. It's simply not a game worth playing.

Principle Three
Keep costs reasonable.

I have been fortunate enough to hear Professor Ken French[20] speak on numerous occasions and even sat next to him at dinner a few years ago.

He is one of the smartest academics in finance today.

He opened his presentation with one picture and summarised his 50 years of work in just a few minutes.

He said "If we assume the market prices are fair, all the players in the market are one big circle. Over time we are all trading against each other in this circle or market.

"Now fund manager A has a cost of 2 per cent and fund manager B has costs of 0.25 per cent.

Who will perform better regardless of skill/expertise?

With absolute certainty, Fund manager B."

Unlike many areas of life, in investments a lower cost manager is actually the best option.

Principle Four
Let markets work for you.

Historically, share, property and bond markets have rewarded investors.

---

20 Kenneth Ronald "Ken" French is the Roth Family Distinguished Professor of Finance at the Tuck School of Business, Dartmouth College. He has also been a faculty member at MIT, the Yale School of Management, and the University of Chicago Booth School of Business.

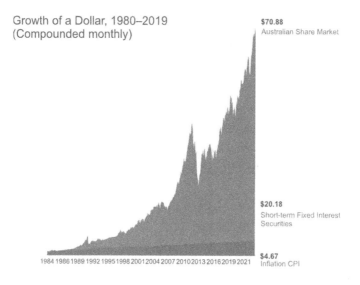

Growth of a Dollar, 1980–2019
(Compounded monthly)

$70.88
Australian Share Market

$20.18
Short-term Fixed Interest
Securities

$4.67
Inflation CPI

1984 1986 1989 1992 1995 1998 2001 2004 2007 2010 2013 2016 2019 2021

Principle Five
Always have enough cash, even if rates are low.

You need cash and fixed interest.

Many people, especially in a low-interest rate environment, say they don't want to hold any cash because the return is too low. By the way, in 2019 bonds had returns of between 5 and 9 per cent — much better than cash.

How much cash should you have?

If retired:

- At least one year of your annual income requirement in cash, some at call, some in a high earning term deposit
- At least three years of this amount and up to five years in term deposits and fixed interest.

In your forties and fifties:

- At least three months' monthly expenses in cash, some at call, some in a high earning term deposit — ideally six months.

Fixed interest also refers to bonds. Bonds are an important asset as they provide income and an insurance buffer when growth markets are volatile,

But don't take a high risk with bonds. Use a diversified approach.

The two factors that determine your return are the maturity and credit ratings.

The safest bonds have a short maturity and a high credit rating.

The interest rate is the best way to gauge the risk you are taking. There is no free lunch.

So an offer on the radio for a high interest 'safe' investment in a mortgage fund offering 8 per cent a year would be very risky.

Principle Six
Diversification works.

Many share portfolios I have seen have poor structure and diversification. For example a $500,000 super fund holding Australian listed shares may look like this:

NAB, $126,000
CBA, $100,000
WOW, $60,000
TLS, $40,000
RIO, $45,000

BHP, $90,000

CYB, $1,500

S32, $500

WES, $25,000

COL, $12,000

Plus a few random picks to round out the portfolio.

Now, I'm not saying any of these companies are doomed. I just don't know.

What I do know is that I would not put all my future income requirements and wealth preservation needs into 10 randomly allocated shares. That is not a sound strategy.

Investing more widely and globally increases the potential return and reduces risk.

Home Market
Index Portfolio

Global Market
Index Portfolio

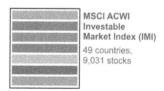

S&P/ASX 300 Index
1 country,
296 stocks

MSCI ACWI
Investable
Market Index (IMI)
49 countries,
9,031 stocks

Principle Seven

Be aware of and manage your emotions when investing.

Daily headlines can unsettle you and make you rethink your strategy. When this happens, make sure you revisit your plan and remember the decades of research that underpins your approach. A daily headline should not make you alter your strategy.

Avoid Reactive Investing

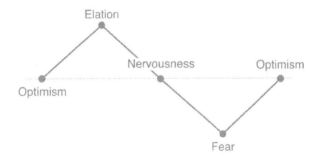

Every time there is a sudden fall in the markets, the headlines the next day will inevitably look like this:

"WORST DAY IN YEARS"

"BILLIONS WIPED OFF SHARES"

And a picture of that same trader looking very worriedly at the screens .

The media have a role, and an important one, in your life, but they are not your investment manager.

There are more good days than bad in markets, but of course you don't see headlines such as

"CALM DAY ON MARKETS, INVESTORS SAFE" very often.

We all know bad news sells and that the editor's job is to sell papers.

The best way to ensure emotions don't get in the way is:

- Have a sensible structure
- Ensure you have enough funds in cash and fixed interest
- Diversify.

Principle Eight
Avoid Market Timing.

You never know which markets will perform when, and there is no evidence of anyone being able to reliably outperform using market timing strategies.

Principle Nine
Follow research and evidence rather than headlines.

Eugene Fama and Kenneth French have developed the three-factor model:

They started by looking at the size of companies and how much a stock's price was above or below its accounting book value and then used this information to divide the market into categories. They took half of the companies, those with the largest market value, and placed them into the large cap category, and the other half was placed in the small cap category. Next, if the company's stock price was relatively high compared to its book value, it was placed in the growth category, and if the stock price was relatively low compared to its book value, it was placed in the value category. They made no attempt to evaluate good or bad companies, or good or bad management. Their decades of research illustrates that across all major markets there has been a significant premium in value and small companies.

Principle Ten
Focus on what you can control.

- Create an investment plan to fit your needs and risk tolerance.
- Structure a portfolio along the dimensions of expected returns.

- Diversify globally.
- Manage expenses, turnover and taxes.
- Stay disciplined through market dips and swings.

Use a defined structure to build a portfolio:
1. Assess your goals and circumstances.
2. Set long-term investment objectives.
3. Plan your asset allocation.
4. Select your investment approach.
5. Build your portfolio.

And a quick reminder about what is unlikely to lead to successful investing:

- Investing using guesswork or forecasts
- Spending more than you earn
- Investing using expensive products
- Investing using the media or newsletters
- Chasing stock pickers or star managers
- Investing in products that no one can explain simply
- Thinking it's different this time
- Hot tips.

Charts sourced from Dimensional Fund Advisors

Afterword

Now that you've read this book you know about a new, different and better way to invest your money. Next, you have three main choices to make:

1. Stay as you are, and leave your superannuation or investments where they are.

2. Implement the book's principles yourself.
    If you need help or additional tools you can contact me at Nigel@scientiam.com.au or via the site www. Scientiam.com.au

3. Use an independent adviser to help you implement your investment strategy, but be sure to follow the principles in this book, as they provide some if not all of the framework for your investment plan.

My own practice, Arch Capital, can assist, or we can direct you to someone in your area.

It's all about sharing the knowledge that you may not have had access to before picking up this book.

Glossary

Active fund - An active fund is the description given to managed funds that apply strategies of stock picking or market timing. They tend to trade frequently and have higher costs than passive managed funds

APRA - Australian Prudential Regulation Authority

ASIC - Australian Securities and Investment Commission

Balanced Fund - An investment fund that has a mix of defensive and growth investments. A balanced fund might look like 40 per cent in cash and bonds, 10 per cent in property, 30 per cent in Australian shares and 20 per cent in international shares.

Bonds - Often called fixed interest or fixed income investments, a bond is an investment where you effectively loan money to a government or company and in return receive interest. The interest may also be referred to as a coupon. A 10-year government bond may pay a coupon or interest rate of 2 per cent.

Contribution Cap - This is the maximum you may contribute to your super account each year.

Diversified Fund - An investment fund that has a mix of defensive and growth investments. A diversified fund might look like 40 per cent in cash and bonds, 10 per cent in property, 30 per cent in Australian shares and 20 per cent in international shares. Similar to a Balanced Fund

Dividend - when a company makes a profit, it may pay a dividend to investors.

Exchange Traded Fund - An ETF is simply a managed fund that can be traded on the stock exchange.

Equities - Another name for shares or stocks that are an investment in a company for which you receive a return via a dividend and potential growth in the share price.

Fund Manager - a company or individual managing investments professionally.

FUM – Funds under management

Growth phase - refers to when you want your portfolio to grow and may be able to accommodate more assets in shares and property

Index Funds - investment funds that aim to match the return of a certain market benchmark

Investment Fee - the dollar and percentage amount charged to your account for the investment service provided

Managed Fund - a managed fund pools together investors' money into a professionally managed investment portfolio that is built and run by a specialist fund manager. The fund's strategy may be based on different asset classes, such as shares, property or fixed interest, or around a particular objective, such as growth or income. Managed funds are unitised, so as an investor you will receive units to reflect your investment. Income is paid as "distributions". Funds either pay investors annually, half-yearly, quarterly or monthly.

MER - Management Expense Ratio. Most fund managers charge a percentage of the assets they manage. This is called a management fee, expressed as a percentage of the MER.

Passive fund - A passive managed fund is the description given to funds that, when compared to active funds, have lower turnover and lower costs. Some passive funds also track an index or benchmark.

PDS - Product Disclosure Statement

Performance fee - a fee charged by a manager when they reach a certain performance hurdle. Scientiam does not use funds that charge a performance fee.

Portfolio - another term used to describe your investments

Preservation age - the age that you can access your superannuation

Unclaimed Super - funds that have not been claimed, if for example someone has moved overseas or simply forgotten about an account. You can search for unclaimed super at australiansuperfinder.com.au.

References

Websites

www.dimensional.com

www.spindices.com/spiva

www.famafrench.dimensional.com

www.evidenceinvestor.com

www.bloomberg.com

Books

"Abundance" Peter H Diamandis

"The Truth About Money" Ric Edleman

"The Barefoot Investor" Scott Pape

"The 7 Habits of Highly Effective People" Stephen R. Covey

"The Investment Answer" Daniel C. Goldie and Gordon S. Murray

"The Smartest investment book You'll ever read" Daniel R. Solin

"Money - Master the game" Tony Robbins

"So you think you are ready to retire" Barry Lavalley

"The Unbeatable Market: Taking the Indexing Path to Financial Peace of Mind" Ron Ross.

"Delivering Certainty" Jim Stackpool

"The Little Book of Common Sense Investing" John C Bogle

"Thinking, fast and slow " Daniel Kahneman

Acknowledgments

I would like to thank Jaqui Lane (jaqui@thebookadviser. com.au) for all her assistance and advice. This is my first book and her input and patience was invaluable. Thank you Jaqui and for removing my fears and doubt as well. I strongly recommend Jaqui to anyone reading this who has thought about writing a book.

Throughout this book I have referenced a lot of material to Dimensional amongst others. I have acknowledged Dimensional and thank them for their material. I also will state that there is and never had been a financial connection between me and Dimensional. I simply believe they do amazing work and strive to make clients lives better by implementing great ideas from finance into accessible funds.

To all that have helped read, provide acknowledgements and advice to get this book through to print thank you.

To my wife Keiva and children Max, Audrey, Oscar and angel Arch, you are everything to me. Writing a book means a few late nights and some weekends researching and editing so thank you for allowing me the time to put all this to paper. I hope it helps my children and theirs in the years to come.

Contacts and Resources

After reading this book, if you are looking for an independent resource to help you implement these ideas you can talk with an independent adviser or use the internet

Here are a few contacts

For personal advice:
Arch Capital www.archcapital.com.au

For online investment information
www.scientiam.com.au

To take control of your finances and learn more about how to invest successfully with an academic advantage, check out www.scientiam.com.au for insights about how markets really work and how as an investor you can learn how to really invest and not gamble.

Appendix

What is an index?

Now you know where returns come from, it's important to understand that all major markets can be benchmarked. Benchmarking is important so you can gauge how your investment is performing in its market.

A benchmark index is a group of securities used to measure the performance of other stocks or securities in the market. The Dow Jones Industrial Average, the S&P 500, and the Russell 2000 are examples of benchmark indices.

There are nearly 3.3 million stock market indices around the world, according to new research from the Index Industry Association (IIA).

Stock market indices measure the value of a section of a country's stock market through a weighted average of selected stocks. These indices help investors and analysts describe the market and compare different investments. Many managed funds and exchange-traded funds (ETFs) attempt to track these indices to provide investors with exposure to a given market.

Examples from around the world include:

China: SSE Composite Index, SZSE
          Component Index, CSI 300 Index

Japan:	Nikkei 225 Index, Topic Index, JPX-Nikkei 400 Index
Germany:	DAX 30 Index, TecDAX Index, MDAX Index
United Kingdom:	FTSE 100 Index, FTSE All-Share Index, FTSE techMark Index
France:	CAC 40 Index, CAC Next 20 Index, CAC Mid 60 Index
India:	Bombay Stock Market Index, National Stock Exchange of India Index, MCX Stock Exchange Index
Italy:	FTSE MIB Index, FTSE Italia Mid Cap Index, MIBTel Index
Brazil:	Bovespa Stock Index, IBrX Stock Index, ITEL Stock Index
Canada:	S&P TSX 60 Index, S&P TSX Composite Index, S&P TSX Venture Composite Index
South Korea:	KOSPI Index, KOSDAQ Index
Australia:	The All Ordinaries, The ASX 300.

When did index investing start?

Index investing was first made broadly available to United States' investors with the launch of the first indexed managed fund in 1976. Since then, low-cost index investing has proven to be a successful investment strategy over the long term, outperforming the majority of other funds across markets and asset styles (S&P Dow Jones Indices, 2015).

In part because of this long-term outperformance, index investing has seen exponential growth among investors, particularly in the United States, and especially since the global financial crisis of 2007–2009.

In recent years, governmental regulatory changes, the introduction of indexed ETFs, and a growing awareness of the benefits of low-cost investing in multiple world markets have made index investing a global trend.

A market-capitalisation-weighted index investment strategy via a managed fund or an ETF seeks to track the returns of a market or markets.

A summary of our asset allocation approach

1. Short-Term: Behavioural Risk
Behavioural Risk is when our emotions convince us to react to market losses or gains.

The first bucket will have a fixed dollar amount to cover the first several years of living costs. It acts as an umbrella for rainy days and provides the peace of mind to stay invested for the long term.

2. Medium-Term: Point-In-Time Risk
Point-In-Time Risk is when a portfolio's value drops when it is time to withdraw money.

The second bucket will have a varying balance that will initially have several more years of living costs, but may rebalance to the growth bucket to avoid the point-in-time risk associated with locking in buckets at the beginning of the retirement period.

3. Long-Term: Longevity Risk

Longevity Risk is living longer than there is money saved for living costs.

The third bucket acts as the engine that enables the portfolio to overcome, or at least offset, the withdrawals.

Retirement Income - Three Buckets

The first bucket will have a fixed dollar amount to cover the first several years of living costs. It acts as an umbrella for rainy days that provides the peace of mind to stay invested for the long term

The second bucket will have a varying balance that will initially have several more years of living costs, but may rebalance to the growth bucket to avoid the point –in–time risk associated with locking in buckets at the beginning of the retirement period.

The third bucket acts as the engine that enables the portfolio to overcome, or at least offset, the withdrawals

We recommend a bucket approach to deal with these three risks.

- Short Term
- Midterm
- Long Term

Short Term	Midterm	Long Term
Behavioral Risk	Point-in-Time & Behavioral Risk	Longevity Risk
3-5 years of spending needs	5-10 years of spending needs	Remainder

Nigel Baker is a 20 year 'veteran' of investment markets who has skilfully guided his clients through many challenges, including the Global Financial Crisis and more recently COVID-19.

During this time, Nigel has provided his clients with steady assurance, following a proven model of investment diversification.

He is a Trusted Adviser to many prominent clients, with a partnership mindset to his clients.

He is a family man, and lives in Newport, NSW Australia with his wife and 4 children.

Troy Marchant CA Partner Advice Co

Nigel Baker has long been a fierce advocate for his profession and the need for clients to be able to simultaneously access advice expertise and financial literacy.

In "The Super Secret" Nigel has successfully removed unnecessary complexity and stripped investing back to its core principles, making this knowledge more accessible for his audience.

Nick Langton, Co-Founder & CEO,
WIMP 2 WARRIOR

This book is an exceptional example of how complex concepts can be explained in simple language, and will be a terrific addition to a marketplace that needs a hand with financial literacy. Nigel's comprehensive technical skills as a Chartered Accountant, coupled with his communication skills gained through being a financial adviser combine brilliantly and shine in the way this book has been presented. Well done, Nigel!

Bronny Speed, BEd Grad Dip Acc FCA CFPLeader –
Financial Advice, Chartered Accountants Australia and
New Zealand, Founding Director – AccountantsIQ Pty Ltd